Behind the Executive Door

Karol M. Wasylyshyn

Behind the Executive Door

Unexpected Lessons for Managing Your Boss and Career

 Springer

Karol M. Wasylyshyn
Philadelphia, USA
kwasylyshyn@erols.com

ISBN 978-1-4614-0375-3   e-ISBN 978-1-4614-0376-0
DOI 10.1007/978-1-4614-0376-0
Springer New York Dordrecht Heidelberg London

Library of Congress Control Number: 2011938233

Printed on acid-free paper

Springer is part of Springer Science+Business Media (www.springer.com)

For Ken,
Ever *Remarkable*

Acknowledgments

I wrote this book while looking out at the sea from my friend Bob Kaeser's getaway home in Cape May Beach, NJ. There is a Buddha resting atop the weathered wood of the deck's surround. It reminded me to B-R-E-A-T-H-E, and to stay calm whenever the words were not coming. Thanks to the generosity of Bob and his partner, Don Stremme, I got to go there in every season – every season for a couple of years trying to pull these words out and to organize them into something potentially helpful to whomever read them. I got to be there when the full moons arrived and spread over the bed as I fell asleep thinking about the words and the difference between when the moon was undiluted and when it was not.

I fell asleep one night near the end of this writing doing math in my head quick calculation of the number of hours in a week: 168. I was reminded of the hundreds of executives who have influenced the writing of this book – they don't sleep much and typically spend most of these 168 hours on work. I express deep gratitude to each of them for they have been my life's work and I have shared their sleeplessness. I have also learned from each of them, and I am especially grateful for their belief in my approach to executive development – an approach that integrates business and psychology in ways that have accelerated their effectiveness as leaders. I treasure the trust we have placed in each other – a trust that has opened the real issues for discussion, learning, and growth.

In addition to my executive clients, I've been rewarded by authentic and lasting partnerships with a number of gifted Human Resources professionals. These partnerships started in 1985 when I met Rohm and Haas (now Dow) Human Resources Director, Mark X. Feck. Mark urged me to create a high potential development process that honored and focused on people holistically – a process that would, in his words, "go inside out." This has influenced all of my work ever since that fateful meeting. After Mark's death, the work at Rohm and Haas carried on through my HR partnerships with Jim Tabb, Marisa Guerin, Joe Forish, and Deb Kurucz.

I have also had memorable collaborations with other distinctive HR professionals to include Hab Butler, Jim Grady, Nancy Marsh, Bob Nalewajek, Mary O'Neill, Cynthia Orme, Frank Smith, and Deb Weinstein. Each in his or her own way guided me into the totems of their organization's cultures and shared full truths about the senior executives whom they entrusted to me for coaching. My collegial conversations and special friendship with Tom Kaney, former Senior Vice President of Human Resources at GlaxoSmithKline, is an ongoing source of inspiration.

Major mentors – David McWhirter, Ulys ("Duke") Yates, and Frank Masterpasqua – continue to influence my thinking and all that has been written here. While David, a psychiatrist, is now deceased, I hold his memory close for without his guidance I would never have pursued a career in psychology. Frank, a brilliant university professor, has become the brother I never had. And the American poet, Duke Yates, has been much to me beyond mentor – boss, surrogate Dad, devoted friend, and poet/collaborator. His astute encouragement – especially of my poetry – has stoked a creative fire between us that includes the writing of a soon-to-be published volume of our joint poems.

There are also inspirational others, rare and treasured friends, to include Paul Koprowski, Monica McGrath, Marilyn Sifford, and Ginny Vanderslice. Their unconditional caring and support of my work has eased the darker days of writing angst – and has inserted a certain glint into the brighter hours.

This book would never exist at all without the efforts of my agent, John Willig. His guidance and belief in this project kept me going through the tougher patches. His gift of a good luck Daruma Doll sits on the desk reinforcing my life mantra revealed recently through the words of another friend, Tom Foley, who once described my life pattern as "dreams with deadlines."

Speaking of deadlines, I extend the warmest gratitude to my Editor, Nick Philipson whose relentless enthusiasm and provision of just the right feedback helped steer this book to its timely completion. Thanks too to his staff member Charlotte Cusumano for her deft efforts.

And finally, I offer a bucket of stars to my star Office Manager, Carol Testa. While I often joke about her being the *real boss*, she *is* a guiding force behind everything I do. She is my face to the world, my gate keeper, my time keeper – and she does it all with uncommon grace, exquisite attentiveness, and good humor. In short, she is *Remarkable* and I strive to be that for her as well as for everyone who has helped me make this book happen.

Philadelphia, PA   Karol M. Wasylyshyn

Prologue

Behind the Executive Door reveals what I've learned about the leadership behavior of top business executives in a broad array of industries throughout the world. What I know is important for *you* to know – assuming you want the time you spend at work to be more rewarding, minimally stressful, and maybe even fun.

There are two objectives of this book. First, to explain executive behavior in a manner that can have palliative effects – especially for people who have struggled with enigmatic and/or bad bosses. And second, to provide guidance for how to manage bosses more effectively, and in doing so advance career prospects as well.

The focus here on *managing one's boss* is a departure from most books about leadership. Those focus on how to become a leader. In *Behind the Executive Door*, we are looking at how to deal with established leaders. I have extrapolated pragmatic advice from my consulting experiences – advice based on understanding of executives' behavior and how this information can aid the people who report to them.

Yes, it is possible to manage a boss – although the specifics of this challenge are more varied than at any other time in business. Your boss may be younger than you, may be a woman, or may be someone from another global sector. You may have a "virtual" reporting relationship to someone you see "live" just a few times a year. You may have more than one boss simultaneously. Whatever the complexities of your boss reality, by the time you finish reading this book, you should know how to do a better job of managing it.

You'll know how to do this *not* because you've been given pat answers, simplistic reasoning, or false encouragement. You'll know how to better manage a boss because you've been given an uncommon look at the characteristic *behavior* of business leaders behind their executive doors. In short, you'll know how to manage bosses better because this behavioral knowledge gives you deeper insights that can inform more successful interactions with them.

Some years ago, I became intrigued by the question of whether or not the most prevalent behaviors of business executives with whom I'd worked represented any particular leadership types. And if they did (they did), I knew this information would be useful to those who work for them, as well as influencing the growth and development of these executives.

I named these three types *Remarkable, Perilous,* and *Toxic.* Surely there are infinite ways to consider leadership types – and an army of consultants to describe them. In other writing about these types I emphasized, "My intent is not to over-simplify or to stereotype leaders or to proffer these types as a definitive representation of leadership styles but rather to pursue a truth known to most who have worked in business organizations: there are great leaders, so-so leaders, and terrible ones, too" (Wasylyshyn, 2011, p. 11).

Behind the Executive Door merges my clinical psychology training and business management background to drive a deep descriptive stake in the sand. From my insider consulting perspective, less obvious truths are conveyed about how business leaders lead, and practical guidance is given about how to leverage these truths.[1]

Bottom line: those who can identify and understand the leadership behaviors of their bosses are more likely to manage them well. Those who lack such understanding are at risk for chronic tension with bosses, frustration, disappointments, misunderstandings – or worse – especially in unstable economic climates.

It is important to note that I have purposely avoided a clinical diagnostic discussion of these leadership types. I believe that that would distract from the core intention of this book: to help people manage whatever type of boss they have – psychologically flawed or gifted. While I am striving to establish a useful descriptive semantic (*Remarkable, Perilous* and Toxic), this is different from a diagnosis and I want to prevent these leader type descriptions from morphing into an unprofessional diagnostic labeling of business leaders.

However, it is true that a number of the executives in my research and consulting practice – especially those whom I place in the *Toxic* leader category – would meet the criteria for diagnosable mental disorders. Much has been written of late about the presence of psychiatrically dysfunctional people in business leadership roles. Ghaemi (2011) suggests that mentally ill leaders can actually function more effectively in times of crisis than can

---

[1] My consulting model is based on long-term relationships with companies that value the interaction between business challenges and a psychologically informed (insight-oriented) approach to effective leadership and leadership development.

psychologically fit leaders. He cites Churchill, Gandhi and Jack Kennedy as prime examples of leaders whose dark depressions were a factor in their leading their respective countries through dark times. Ronson (2011) maintains that some business leaders like Al "Chainsaw" Dunlap would score high on indicators of psychopathy. These indicators include superficial charm, grandiosity, manipulation, lack of empathy, and impulsivity.

The clinically-trained reader will be able to make diagnostic discernments based on the information in BEHIND THE EXECUTIVE DOOR. However, I repeat that the main event of this book is to provide behavior clues for the rapid recognition of leaders' styles – not their diagnoses. I believe this recognition will inform effective ways of managing bosses of all types – and by extension – effective boss management has positive implications for navigating successful careers.

Part I of *Behind the Executive Door* provides information for a fuller understanding of business executive behavior. In Chap. 1, I describe the initial case analysis that resulted in my identification of the three leadership types – *Remarkable, Perilous,* and *Toxic* – and the subsequent research that has shown these types to be empirically distinct. Further, I remain mindful of individual differences, i.e., not all leaders fall neatly into one of these three categories nor are they indelibly locked into any one of them. Therefore, I have conceptualized executives as moving along this behavioral continuum of three leadership types – *Remarkable, Perilous,* and *Toxic.*

On any given day, as with professional athletes, where a leader falls on this continuum will be influenced by the confluence of work and personal factors. Bad business results, failed projects, flawed strategies, marital discord, health problems, the illnesses of family members, and other familial distractions are some of the factors that can throw even the most *Remarkable* leader off stride. The key to managing bosses well is the ability to recognize where they are on the Remarkable, Perilous, and Toxic behavior continuum.

This recognition can influence the in-the-moment adjustments regarding how to interact with them, i.e., such recognition can help ensure one *meets them where they need to be met*. This is fundamental to managing bosses effectively.

There are also shades of difference among the types (see Fig. 1 – Leadership Type Continuum). Within the context of this leadership typology, these shades of difference in leaders' behavior warrant further research.

Chapters 2–4 provide the descriptions of each type based on life histories, case notes, anecdotal and empirical research, psychological testing data, and organization-based interviews.

The Leadership Type Exercise provided in Chap. 5 has been designed to pinpoint boss leadership behavior based on the three types described in previous chapters. While this is no more than a preliminary survey of boss leadership behavior, it will prove a useful starting point for exploring the lessons in subsequent chapters. (Readers might also use this survey as a self-assessment thus comparing boss and self leader types.)

Part II is devoted to applying the understanding of business leaders' behavior. Road-tested lessons are provided – lessons that influenced the most progress among executive clients whom I coached, especially those who were focused on maximizing relationships with *their* bosses. In *Behind the Executive Door*, these lessons are recast to stimulate your thoughts about managing the boss or bosses with whom you interact at work.

Chapters 6–8 are devoted to the specific lessons for managing *Remarkable, Perilous,* and *Toxic* bosses, respectively.

In a stark but potentially intriguing departure from the rest of this book, Chap. 9 draws upon metaphor as a catalyst for further reflection about leadership behavior. Specifically, examples of business executives are condensed into free verse. Here, the interpretations of leadership behavior are left to the reader – but ample guidance also accompanies each vignette. These poems – or executive vignettes as I sometimes refer to them – are intended to intensify one's recollections of *Remarkable, Perilous,* and *Toxic* bosses, as well as to sharpen one's ability to recognize these boss types in present and future work situations.

The Epilogue provides a final weaving of this enriched understanding of three prevalent leader types with the *unexpected lessons* for managing bosses who represent these types. Surely managing a boss more effectively can accelerate greater contentment and career success in the short term. However, this achievement can also influence growth that is more personal and enduring.

Kafka reportedly said, "A good novel is a blow to the head." While not fiction, *Behind the Executive Door* is intended as a blow to the head given its relentless truth-telling and insights about business leaders' behavior. At the same time, the immediacy and visceral quality of these leader type descriptions and illustrations can provide the voyeuristic pleasure of fiction. Enjoy. Learn. Internalize.

Philadelphia, PA   Karol M. Wasylyshyn

Contents

UNDERSTANDING THE BEHAVIOR OF BUSINESS LEADERS

The How of Leadership … An Era of Intense Behavior Scrutiny

> *One place that we have not yet quantified, systematized, or commoditized, one which, in fact, cannot be commoditized or copied: the realm of human behavior – HOW we do what we do.*
>
> *Dov Seidman,*
> *Chairman and CEO, LRN*

In *Behind the Executive Door*, the *how* of leadership refers to the *human behavior* dimension of executives' effectiveness or lack of same. Business historians will remember the late twentieth and early twenty-first centuries as a time of intense leader scrutiny – not only of their results but of *how* executives pursued those results. Currently, not even the most impressive business results will transcend considerations of leaders' managerial, moral, and ethical behavior.

The truth of this was vividly revealed early in the year 2000 in the wake of a number of major corporate and accounting scandals in companies that included Enron, Tyco Int'l, Adelphia, and WorldCom. The ethical leadership lapses in these organizations cost investors billions of dollars and exposed significant problems regarding conflicts of interest and incentive compensation packages. These corporate and accounting scandals brought down global accounting firm Arthur Andersen, sent Enron executives Jeffrey Skilling and Andrew Fastow to prison, and influenced the creation of the Sarbanes–Oxley Act of 2002, commonly referred to as SOX. While there has been ongoing debate about the costs of this act, it ushered in a new era of enhanced standards for all US public company boards and public accounting, as well as the intensified behavioral scrutiny of C-level executives.

During the last four decades, an astounding mix of socioeconomic and political forces has transformed the place we call work. These forces include the explosion of information technology, business globalization, the surge

K.M. Wasylyshyn, *Behind the Executive Door: Unexpected Lessons for Managing Your Boss and Career*, DOI 10.1007/978-1-4614-0376-0_1,
© Karol M. Wasylyshyn 2012

in youthful entrepreneurism and wealth, increasing gender parity in the workplace, two-career couples, role reversal marriages, open workplace seating plans, pets at work, virtual employees, the exponential power of social engagement technology in commerce, and the threat of terrorism, too. That the confluence of these developments – in addition to the ethical issues cited above – would have significant implications for what constitutes effective leadership was inevitable.

Effective modern-day leaders would necessarily have evolved from Maccoby's (1976) conceptualization of the "gamesman." Of this type of leader he wrote, "In contrast to the jungle-fighter industrialists of the past, he is driven not to build or to preside over empires, but to organize winning teams. Unlike the security-seeking organization man, he is excited by the chance to cut deals and to gamble. Although more cooperative and less hardened than the autocratic empire builder and less dependent than the organization man, he is more detached and emotionally inaccessible than either. And he is troubled by it; the new industrial leader can recognize that his work develops his head but not his heart" (pp. 31–32).

Effective modern-day leaders have evolved to what I call the *total brain leader* (Wasylyshyn 2011b). These leaders have integrated their left-brain cognitive abilities (the what) with right-brain conceptual and relationship talents (the how). They apply their *what* and *how* leadership assets to win in a Darwinian global business climate. These are the courageous visionaries too impatient to wait and resilient enough to adjust when necessary. These leaders have grown up in teams and have natural instincts for forming high-performing groups that help them blaze new ground and/or discover niches of rewarding business pursuits. They are cutting bolder deals and gambling faster in a business atmosphere where the combination of anticipation, speed, and execution rules.

And perhaps the most distinctive factor of today's new leaders – these total brain leaders – is that they are not as detached and emotionally inaccessible as their business predecessors. Since Goleman's (1996) ground-breaking book on emotional intelligence, the business world has socialized and rewarded a new leadership breed. These leaders are more self-aware, use their emotions, display empathy, and form relationships that are not just transactional. They are, in fact, evolving both head and heart simultaneously.

These leaders are scary bright, bursting with business acumen, and emotionally smart, too. These intellectual–emotional hybrid leaders inspire the efforts of others, sustain motivation, and enjoy the consistent respect and commitment of people throughout their organizations.

In writing about the new breed of top executive Groysberg, Kelly and MacDonald (2011) state, "… requirements for all C-level jobs have shifted toward business acumen and 'softer' leadership skills ... to thrive as a C-level executive, an individual needs to be a good communicator, a collaborator, and a strategic thinker" (p. 68). While content is central in effective communication and collaboration, the behavioral *how* requirements for listening well and being stellar team players are inescapable.

Increasingly, prestigious business schools are having to adapt their curricula to respond to current leadership demands. In a 2011 interview with the Wall Street Journal, Thomas S. Robertson, Dean of the Wharton Business School, reflected, "If you talk to alumni 20 years out they say, 'Ooh boy, I wish I had gotten more in the way of leadership skills – how to manage other people'... the set of technical skills that gets them the job, becomes less important as they get into middle and senior management" (Korn 2011, para. 22).

Economist and futurist Jeremy Rifkin (2009) wrote, "The empathic civilization is emerging. A younger generation is fast extending its empathic embrace beyond religious affiliations and national identification to include the whole of humanity and the vast project of life that envelops the earth" (p. 616). While Rifkin's fear regarding planetary collapse due to climate change before we reach a point of global connectivity may or may not be warranted, his concept of the emergence of an *empathic civilization* is right on point. It has immediate applicability for current leaders – and our understanding of them.

Through the leadership lens of empathy,[1] we have witnessed the early career flameouts of some very gifted leaders lacking in this dimension of leadership. Despite his string of double-digit growth quarters, Mark Hurd, the former CEO of Hewlett-Packard, behaved with indignance and denial in the wake of the HP board's scrutiny of his questionable expense reports and alleged personal improprieties. This behavior accelerated the Board's decision to fire him.

While Tony Hayward, former CEO of BP, mostly inherited the problems that lead to the devastating 2010 oil spill in the Gulf of Mexico, his insensitive comments and behavior in the wake of it cost him his job. Paul Sonne of the Wall Street Journal (7/26/10) wrote, "Mr. Hayward's various gaffes – saying he wanted his 'life back' – and sour appearance before legislators showed a degree of tone deafness that is no longer acceptable for corporate leaders."

In addition to emotional tone deafness, other behavioral problems – sexual and ethical – have lead to the derailments of a number of political figures, including John Edwards, Rep. Charles B. Rangel, Eliot Spitzer, and Ex-Governor Rod Blagojevich.

In the international political arena, 2011 brought the stunning ouster of Egypt's President Hosni Mubarak who had ruled that country for 30 years.

In an 18-day bloodless revolt, the people clamored for a democratic election process and greater economic opportunity in a country rife with corruption and where the majority of citizens lived on two US dollars a day. Described as disciplined, hard-working, but without charm, Mubarak had come to rely on a fearsome police apparatus to retain his tight control of the country. While the early years of his rule helped maintain some degree of stability in the Middle East, he was greatly flawed in the leadership *how* perspective described aptly in one news story as an "isolated autocratic."

A better *how* personality emerged through the Egyptian protest and eventual ouster of its autocratic ruler – Wael Ghomin – described by the media as the "reluctant hero" of Tahrir Square. Ghomin, a Google Marketing Manager in Egypt, was emboldened by Egyptians' angst, deprivation, and courage and made an impassioned plea on public television for Mubarak's resignation. An example of sudden, situational, and EQ-attuned leadership, Ghomin stood in stunning contrast to the charmless and disconnected autocrat, Mubarak.

In the winter of 2011, thousands of Italian women protested throughout their country, demanding that Prime Minister Silvio Berlusconi resign in the wake of his patronizing a female minor for sex and abusing his powers in an attempt to cover up this relationship. Whether these allegations were true or not, the scandal intensified Berlusconi's preexisting troubles with the law and galvanized a nationwide movement calling for greater dignity and rights for women. From a leadership *how* perspective, Berlusconi's well-known flirtations with women and public comments such as "…it's better to be passionate about beautiful women than to be gay" further underscored his limitations as a leader.

In the American business climate of behavior scrutiny, there is increasingly little tolerance for arrogant – albeit talented – business leaders. While strong business results have to be there, they no longer transcend everything else. Leaders who are not mindful of their "how," i.e., leaders who run roughshod over others, commit ethical lapses, or otherwise misbehave, risk their jobs – despite solid business performance.

At the same time, there are impressive examples of senior leaders who get the "how" of leadership and have integrated this with other business talents. These leaders include Howard Schultz, Chairman, President, and CEO of Starbucks, who believes great leaders are sturdy enough to display their vulnerability. In his words, "…that [displaying vulnerability] will bring people closer to you and show people the human side of you" (Bryant 2010, para. 41).

Steve Stefano (2005), the inspirational Managing Partner of Synopia Rx, wrote, "People don't really care what you know until they know you care"

(p. 5). Gifted leaders like Stefano employ what Daniel Goleman et al. (2002) referred to as empathic resonance. In their words, "The fundamental task of leaders is to prime good feeling in those they lead. That occurs when a leader creates resonance – a reservoir of positivity that frees the best in people. At its root, then, the primal job of leadership is emotional" (p. ix).

Jim Collins's (2001) formulation of "level 5" leadership is, at its core, a behavioral depiction of successful leadership, i.e., of getting the "how" right. He wrote, "Level 5 leaders embody a paradoxical mix of personal humility and professional will. They are ambitious, to be sure, but ambitious first and foremost for the company, not themselves" (p. 39).

In this era of behavior scrutiny, *how leaders behave* has assumed prominence on a par with *what they know* related to marketplace dynamics, innovative technologies, strategy mapping, people management, and myriad other factors essential for commercial success. Smart companies like pharmaceutical giant GlaxoSmithKline and DuPont have integrated the *what* and *how* of leadership to design talent management processes that are equally focused on both.[2]

Despite increased Board and media focus on the *how* of leadership and on greater company efforts to assess leadership behavior, development initiatives still lag behind the need of leaders to evolve in this way. Competency-based leadership development activities can get stuck in a time warp where business skill-oriented competencies dominate. These activities are more weighted toward the "hard" leadership competencies – the *what* leaders need to do (e.g., strategic thinking, setting direction, managing innovation, developing others, driving results, etc.) to succeed. While these competencies are critical, they need to be balanced with "soft" interpersonal capabilities – the *how* leaders need to be (e.g., self-aware, emotionally controlled, attuned to others, able to foster strong relationships with all stakeholder groups) to maintain sustained success.

This is an interesting paradox, isn't it? We're in a business climate that is scrutinizing the good and bad aspects of its leaders' behavior to a greater degree than ever before, and yet, company developmental opportunities are not fully in synch with this need. This is one of the key reasons executive coaching has become such a hot niche among leadership development offerings. According to the International Coaches Federation (ICF), there are over 10,000 coaches globally.

But not everyone is afforded the costly opportunity of working with an executive coach. On some level then, *Behind the Executive Door* is a practical leadership "how" tool for a broader population. With the leader "how" information provided here, readers can identify boss types and accelerate their efforts to better manage them, gain insights about their own potential as leaders, and navigate their careers accordingly.

The Emergence of Three Leadership Types

After nearly 30 years of consulting to business executives, I became intrigued by the question: *Do these business leaders represent any particular patterns of behavior?* In an attempt to answer this question, I spent several months analyzing the data in 300 executive coaching cases. Three distinct patterns of behavior emerged with an almost astonishing clarity. Given their most distinct behavioral qualities, I originally named these leadership types Unusual, Unrequted, and Uninterested. Currently, these types are named *Remarkable*, *Perilous*, and *Toxic*.

Since my executive coaching model is based on the integration of historical, psychological, and organization-based data, these files were rich with material to analyze.[3] This analysis was based on the following (1) a life history, (2) psychological assessment tests, (3) leadership competency data (drawn through 360 feedback interviews), and (4) coaching notes.

Life History

A client's life history is taken in a face-to-face meeting lasting approximately 3–4 hours. The client is told that my intention is to track how he/she moved through specific life stages of development because key life themes have implications for leadership effectiveness. Theoretically, this life history taking is influenced most by the psychosocial development theory of twentieth-century Danish German development psychologist and psychoanalyst Erik Erikson.[4] Erikson's theory is based on eight successive life stages with specific development tasks to be accomplished in each stage.

In Stage 1, occurring between birth and age 1, the developmental task is the establishment of trust. When this stage has unfolded well, the child develops trust because physical and emotional needs have been met by caregivers. When it does not go well, a child mistrusts the likelihood that his/her needs will be satisfied, and this can have adverse implications for all relationships thereafter.

Marvin's mother had suffered a serious postpartum depression for several months after his birth. The negative effects of her "absence" from him during the first months of his life were exacerbated by a familial atmosphere bereft of any physical or verbal expression of affection. In his unconscious search for love and human connection – a search compromised by his inability to be truly intimate with anyone – he acted out sexually as an adolescent and embarked upon a lifelong pattern of predatory and/or flirtatious relationships with both men and women.

Inevitably disappointed in people, he could instantaneously turn on or reject others – even those who had been close to him. As a business man, he was admired for his innate intelligence and strategic and operational capabilities, but as a leader, he was described by the people who reported to him as "cold, aloof, and unpredictable." His harsh and sudden criticisms of others' work and/or their intentions often bordered on paranoia, further intensifying their distrust of him and eroding the potential for team alignment and camaraderie.

In Stage 2, occurring between ages 1 and 3, the developmental task is to begin to individuate and explore the world with comfortable feelings of independence. When this stage goes well, the child develops the will and the determination to exercise freedom of choice even in the face of others' demands, resistance, and/or disagreement. When it does not, the person can flounder later in life and be prone toward feelings of shame and doubt.

Maria was the only girl of seven children in an Irish-American family where distinguishing one's accomplishments was essential for both respect and "air time" at the dinner table – center stage of her family's dramatic unfolding. Diminished by the favoritism and academic opportunities afforded to her brothers, she receded into the background until she "escaped" from home immediately after high school. Later in life, she earned impressive academic credentials and embarked upon a notably successful career. However, even then, self-doubt could creep in, and her inclinations to please or to maintain harmony could overshadow or compromise the aggressive pursuit of her own preferences.

In Stage 3, occurring between ages 3 and 5, the developmental task is to start taking initiative in pursuit of specific objectives. When this phase goes well, the child experiences a budding sense of purpose and feels encouraged to pursue certain goals. Things go awry for children who are punished for their independent strivings, and feelings of guilt are internalized deeply. These feelings can have limiting effects later in life, especially in terms of one acting with courage and single-minded drive toward accomplishment.

Growing up poor in the urban northeast, Karen spent the first 10 years of her life without toys and living in a dark cold water flat. With her mother's encouragement to "be different" and overt pride in Karen's ability to "create something from nothing," she spent her preschool years constructing a magical world in a kitchen corner tented with an old sheet and populated by pots, other cooking utensils, and colorful scraps of fabric from the floor around her mother's sewing machine. As an adult, Karen would attribute her ability to generate bold and creative ideas – in both her entrepreneurial business and personal life – to her mother's emotional support and urging for her to set distinctive goals.

In Stage 4, occurring between ages 6 and 11, the major developmental task is to recognize one's brain power as a core and reliable tool for accomplishment. When this phase unfolds well, children develop cognitive competence and experience a growing confidence in the ability to complete tasks of their own choosing. If this stage does not go well, feelings of inferiority and inadequacy can take hold and sabotage the likelihood of a productive future.

Never acknowledged for his excellent academic performance or encouraged to attend college by his working-class parents, Fred was a late bloomer intellectually. Fortunately, he identified the behavioral sciences as a compelling area of professional pursuit, completed a doctoral degree, and flourished in a career distinguished by his outstanding teaching, mentoring, research, and publications. However, despite his enormous capabilities and success, he was prone toward bouts of depression during which crushing feelings of inadequacy could wash over him with tidal effects.

In Stage 5, occurring between ages 12 and 18, the major developmental task is to form a strong sense of identity, i.e., a stable identity that reinforces certainty about the potential for a happy and fruitful life. When this phase unfolds badly, people are vulnerable for what Erikson termed an "identity crisis" that can be characterized by the inability to discover and pursue a meaningful career path and a variable sense of accountability to others.

John was the youngest in an Irish family of eight children. With an absent father and a mother overwhelmed by the day-to-day demands of trying to keep the family together, John was, as he described it, "pretty much lost in the shuffle." Innately bright but bored in his classes, John dropped out of high school. A gifted musician, he became part of Boston's alternative art scene where he created and directed a number of stage productions. He worked odd jobs to support himself and eventually married in his 30s and started a family. With minimal education, no real professional identity, and an anomalous portfolio of work experiences, he would struggle his entire life to retain work and earn enough income to meet his financial responsibilities.

In Stage 6, occurring between ages 18 and 35, the major developmental task is intimacy (1) intimacy in terms of finding and settling into consistent work pursuits and (2) the intimacy of merging with others in sustained love relationships. If things do not go well in this development stage, individuals can drift aimlessly, never finding work about which they are truly passionate and become socially isolated or chronically lonely, given their failure to fuse themselves in love with another.

When Eliot was a freshman in college, the stress of that development passage caused an emotional breakdown that led to his withdrawal from school. Soon thereafter, he enrolled in a prestigious arts school and completed his undergraduate degree there. However, wracked by anxieties, his punishing perfectionism, and incessant self-criticism, he was not able to settle into a career or serious love relationship. None of his efforts to receive psychological help could pull him out of his emotional abyss. Eventually, he was diagnosed as having bipolar illness, began taking medication, and started working at a local coffee café as a first step toward supporting himself and creating a social network.

In Stage 7, occurring approximately between the ages of 35 and 55, the developmental challenge is *generativity*, i.e., finding ways to guide the next generation, to promote the development and well-being of others, and to feel the exhilaration of applying one's knowledge and experiences in ways that are instructive and meaningful. If this does not occur, feelings of worthlessness and/or meaninglessness can fester and lead to an existential depression. Some individuals will use alcohol or other drugs to anesthetize themselves against this psychological pain, thus further isolating themselves from constructive steps forward.

Unable to rise to the challenges of this life stage, some can experience what Erikson termed "stagnation" or become narcissistically self-preoccupied. In short, a rewarding sense of generativity is the major predictor of one's ability to be engaged in the world in caring and productive ways through the adult years.

Having achieved his goal of becoming CEO of a global company by age 50, Peter relished the opportunity to promote its rapid growth through a number of deft and carefully orchestrated strategic decisions and the implementation of key objectives. Similar to other successful CEOs, he was impatient for this growth, but he remained steady and clear enough to channel that impatience in productive ways that helped sustain momentum toward success. Unlike other CEOs, he did not see his tenure in this role as the capstone to his career. Rather, he saw it as a chapter that he would write well – even as he began writing the next one in his head. In the meantime, what gave him the most satisfaction was his mentoring actions that ensured the next generation of leadership within the company – including his successor.

Stories of the Redemptive Self

McAdams (2006) has written about the "redemptive self" as an individual difference among some people in their adult years. He states, "Research has also suggested that highly generative American adults tend to construct self-defining life stories (narrative identities) that feature the psychological theme of redemption – the deliverance from suffering to an enhanced status or position in life ... through stories of redemption, narrators often articulate how they believe they experienced a 'second chance' in life" (p. 81).

In the sports world, Philadelphia Eagles quarterback Michael Vick exemplifies a redemptive tale. Imprisoned 21 months for his involvement in a dogfighting ring, his professional athletic career was seriously sidelined. However, upon his release from prison, Eagles Coach Andy Reid recruited him to Philadelphia. Grateful for his second chance, Vick made public contrition, embarked upon rigorous training, and eventually distinguished himself on the field. In 2011 the Eagles gave Vick a six-year $100 million contract. Through The Vick Foundation, he continues to support at-risk youth in after school programs in Metro Atlanta, and he set up a scholarship fund for surviving victims of the 2010 Virginia Tech shooting tragedy.

In the business realm, Martha Stewart was imprisoned for 5 months for securities fraud. After her release, she steadily rebuilt the Martha Stewart brand by returning to television, publishing more homemaking books, and getting mass retailers, such as Wal-Mart, to stock her line of home furnishings. In addition to her commercial endeavors, she established the Martha Stewart Center for Living at Mount Sinai in New York City – considered to be the #1 geriatrics program in the United States.

Both Vick and Stewart rose from their respective ashes and persevered to find ways to channel their core abilities – and to give back to others as well. Their stories exemplify the self-actualization of gifted people who had been misguided or went astray. Their stories are also universal – triumph out of despair, heroes moving forward with resilience and renewed confidence, transcending barriers and finding new paths leading to productive and inspirational destinations for others as well as for themselves. And while their stories may seem an odd admixture of narcissism and altruism, they are, nevertheless, inspirational stories in which redeemed people find paths into the future that is hopeful and charitable. In this way, they can serve as powerful role models for others.

In Stage 8, beginning approximately at age 55 and continuing until death, the development hurdle is about ego integrity, i.e., achieving an integrated sense of one's self and life events and/or achievements. Can one reflect on his/her life with a sense satisfaction? Do feelings of peace and calm predominate? When dissatisfaction, hostility, and/or restlessness predominate, individuals can fall into a deep sense of despair, looking back on their lives with gnawing feelings of unrequitedness, anger, and frustration.

Having spent his professional life as a well-respected science editor and writer, Dave retired from publishing contented in what he had done, the careers of others whom he had influenced well, and the last phase of it in which he had created a number of impressive medical publications. He was also passionate about what lay ahead – his return to creative writing that included something he had abandoned for 40 years: poetry. Within several years, his poems had been published in many notable American and United Kingdom literary journals. At this writing, he is well into his 80s – still writing poetry, reading voraciously, and, every Sunday afternoon, reciting from memory all the parts in the Shakespearean play he chose for that week.

Psychological Assessment Tools/Preliminary Research Findings

The battery of psychological assessment tools used in my coaching engagements consisted of a combination of *state* and *trait* tests.[5] A total of five psychological assessment tools are used in this battery (1) Watson–Glaser Critical Thinking Appraisal (state), (2) Myers–Briggs Type Indicator (trait), (3) Life Styles Inventory, LSI 1 (state), (4) Revised NEO Personality Inventory (trait), and (5) Bar-On Emotional Quotient Inventory – the EQ-i (state).

The Watson–Glaser measures the ability to reason analytically and logically. The Myers–Briggs provides a profile of behavior preferences. The Life Styles Inventory shows how one's thinking affects behavior as a manager of others. Based on the Big Five Factor theory of personality, the NEO PI-R profiles these five factors (neuroticism, extraversion, openness, agreeableness, and conscientiousness) plus the coordinated subscales for each of the Big 5 factors.[6] Finally, the EQ-i is a measure of emotional intelligence based on five primary scales – intrapersonal EQ, interpersonal EQ, stress management, adaptability, and general mood, plus coordinated subscales for each of these dimensions.[7]

Recent research (by Wasylyshyn, Shorey and Chaffin yet to be published) has shown the three leader types *Remarkable*, *Perilous*, and *Toxic* to be empirically distinct on two of the aforementioned psychological assessment measures. These measures are the NEO PI-R and the EQ-i. In this research, 100 participants were selected from a pool of executives who had received executive assessment (including the NEO PI-R and EQ-i) and coaching services from the lead author between 1982 and 2010. Each participant was mailed a letter explaining that the lead author had developed a leader typology based on her work with them.

This research was carried out to determine if independent investigators – investigators who did not have knowledge of the description of each of the leader types – could identify specific patterns of responses on the NEO and EQ-i scales that would psychometrically differentiate the types. These investigators received the raw NEO and EQ-i data and a number indication for which category the lead author determined each executive to represent. These categories were not however labeled, and the investigators could not determine the characteristics of the groups while assessing the NEO and EQ-i data.

Based on this data, the independent researchers (Shorey and Chaffin) developed the following descriptions of each of the groups.

Remarkable

This group was found to have the most adaptive functioning and best adjustment. They were also found to have generally good moods – upbeat, confident, poised, and outgoing. They are drawn to achieving goals. They enjoy working with and being around others, and they prefer being busy. In their relationships, they are assertive but also skillful in managing them.

Perilous

Compared to *Remarkable* leaders, these individuals were found less likely to have good moods and were less self-confident. They were less likely to work fastidiously or without distraction, and they were less inclined to seek out others. Further, they were more likely (than *Remarkables*) to feel overwhelmed or ineffective under stress. Compared to *Toxic* leaders, they were less likely to be modest and more likely to be secretive or insincere in their dealings with others. They were found to be the most anxious and preoccupied with relationships of all three leader types. It appears that problems in relationships are fueled by their narcissistic needs, suspiciousness of others, and preoccupations with themselves.

Toxic

Compared to *Remarkable* leaders, these executives were found to be less happy and have greater difficulty adapting to new challenges. They are less confident than *Remarkable* leaders, prefer a slower pace, and may have trouble motivating themselves to work hard or stay disciplined. They have more difficulty in their social relationships, and of the three leader types, they are the most interpersonally avoidant. Therefore, they are less likely to seek out others and can be less assertive. They can be more direct, honest, and modest than *Perilous* leaders.

On the EQ-i, *Remarkable* leaders scored higher than both *Perilous* and *Toxic* leaders in General Mood. Between *Remarkable* and *Toxic* leaders, this difference was due to the General Mood subscale of Happiness, but the Optimism subscale showed no significant difference between *Remarkable* and *Toxic* leaders. However, because there was no significant difference between *Remarkable* and *Perilous* on Happiness or Optimism, it seems that these two subscales have a combined effect on the difference between groups 1 and 2 scores in General Mood.

Not surprising, *Remarkable* leaders scored higher than *Toxic* leaders on the Interpersonal subscale of the Interpersonal dimension and higher on the Flexibility subscale of the Adaptability dimension. It would seem that *Remarkable* leaders are better able than *Toxic* ones to manage effective and cooperative interpersonal relationships and they are also generally better able to enact or deal with change, as compared to *Toxic* leaders.

On the Big Five Factors of personality, as measured by the NEO PI-R (see Table 1.1 for definitions of these five factors), *Remarkable* leaders

Table 1.1 Big Five factors of personality as measured by the NEO-PI-R.

Neuroticism	Tendency to experience predominately negative affects (e.g. fear, sadness, anger, guilt, etc.) especially under stress
Extraversion	Inclination toward people; assertive, active, talkative
Openness	Curiosity about inner and outer worlds; willingness to entertain novel ideas and unconventional values
Agreeableness	Altruistic orientation; sympathetic to others; willingness to help; not self-centered
Conscientiousness	Self-control in terms of planning, organizing, execution, task achievement

scored significantly higher than either *Perilous* or *Toxic* leaders on the Extraversion and Conscientiousness domains. While *Perilous* leaders scored higher than *Remarkables* on Neuroticism, neither of these groups was significantly different from *Toxic* leaders on this dimension.

Shorey emphasizes, "In examining the results of the NEO-PI-R, it is important to drill down to the subscale level, because each domain of the Big Five encompasses several constructs which can complicate the interpretation of their umbrella domains."

For example, while it is accurate to say that *Perilous* leaders had higher levels of Neuroticism than *Remarkable* leaders, it is more precise to state that *Perilous* leaders scored higher on the Neuroticism subscale of Vulnerability than *Remarkable* leaders did. Vulnerability is defined by the test creators as a feeling of inability to cope with stress or a feeling of dependency or hopelessness.

On overall Extraversion, *Remarkable* leaders scored higher than both *Perilous* and *Toxic* leaders; however, it was the subscale of Gregariousness (preference for the company of others) that most influenced this result. Further, *Remarkables* were higher than *Toxic* leaders on the Assertiveness and Activity subscales of Extraversion. In short, it appears that *Remarkable* leaders prefer a faster pace than may *Toxic* leaders.

Remarkable leaders scored significantly higher than *Perilous* leaders on three facets of the Conscientiousness factor. These facets are (1) Competence (belief in one's capabilities and efficacy), (2) Dutifulness (adherence to ethical or moral obligations), and (3) Self-Discipline (ability to complete tasks despite distractions). *Remarkable leaders* also scored higher than *Toxic* leaders on the Competence and Self-Discipline subscales of the Conscientiousness factor.

Perilous and *Toxic* leaders differed significantly from each other on only two scales measured by the NEO PI-R. Both of these scales were facets of the Agreeableness factor of the Big Five. Specifically, *Toxic* leaders were significantly higher than *Perilous* leaders in Straightforwardness and Modesty. While straightforwardness can be understood in the context of *Toxic* leaders who can be brash, brutally honest, attacking, or otherwise verbally aggressive, the Modesty finding is anomalous and warrants further exploration. One possible explanation would be that given the self-report nature of the NEO PI-R, the relative lack of self-awareness among many *Toxic* leaders might skew in the direction of modesty, but this finding requires further scrutiny.

Leadership Competency Data

The practice of gathering what has come to be known in organizations as "360 data" has been commonplace for at least two decades.[8] The author typically customizes an interview protocol to be used in interviews with a client sample of 360 participants. For executive clients, this interview protocol always focuses on the key development areas of the business leader as well as on drawing information on essential leadership competencies and behaviors.

The leader competencies, or the *what* dimension, of leadership data used in the derivation of the *Remarkable*, *Perilous*, and *Toxic* leadership types were Strategy, Driving Results, Managing People, and Executive Credibility.[9] The construct of emotional intelligence – including its four dimensions of self-observation, self-management, attunement to others, and relationship traction – was used to draw relevant information for the behavioral or *how* dimension of leadership (see Table 1.2).

Remarkable leaders are typically strong on all four leadership competencies. They are, for the most part, equally strong on the four SO SMART® dimensions of emotional intelligence.[10] In other words, their integration of the *what* demands of leadership (leadership competencies) with the *how* demands of leadership (behavior as influenced by emotions) is the differentiating factor in their effectiveness as leaders. This is described in Chap. 2.

Perilous leaders present a mixed and inconsistent picture as related to both leadership competencies and behaviors. This is explained in Chap. 3.

Given their psychological issues, *Toxic* leaders can manifest serious problems in terms of both leadership competencies and behaviors. Their problems are of a magnitude that they can significantly erode the success of a business. A close look at this flawed leadership type is provided in Chap. 4.

Coaching Notes

First, a caveat: effective coaching needs to be grounded on a foundation of multifaceted data (as described above). Further, this data needs to be distilled into key findings and tracked during the course of coaching so client and coach alike have a clear sense of progress being made – or not.

Table 1.2 Definition of terms

What is emotional intelligence (EQ)?

The awareness of one's own and others' emotions and the ability to discriminate among them. The ability to use that emotional awareness to achieve work and personal objectives

Four dimensions of EQ – SO SMART®

I. Self-observation (SO)	*II. Self-management* (SM)
The awareness and understanding of our emotions and moods – and their effects on others	The ability to control emotions, and to channel them as a resource for achieving work and life objectives
• Awareness of own and others' emotions • Accurate self-assessment	• Self-control and discipline • Trustworthiness & integrity • Resilience • Motivation, bias for action
Core ability: perceiving emotions	Core ability: managing emotions
III. Attunement (to others) (A)	*IV. Relationship traction* (RT)
A genuine focus on others' concerns. Being tuned into organization culture factors. The ability to use emotions in sound problem-solving	The capacity to form relationships that are "real" not just transactional. Influential and consistent leadership. Sufficient emotional understanding to build collaborative teams that deliver results
• Focus on others • Empathy • Ability to build trust • Coaching skill • Organization awareness	• Authenticity • Influence skill • Consistency • Meaningful connections with others • Collaborative teamwork
Core ability: using emotions	Core ability: understanding emotions

---

Another tool for making the coaching work concrete and for tracking its progress is the *Visual Leadership Metaphor*.[11] At the outset of the coaching engagement, executives are asked to describe themselves in very visual terms – terms that capture how they perceive themselves as leaders (1) currently, (2) in transition toward their desired state, and (3) desired/future state. This language is captured by the coach who then collaborates with an artist to produce the three-state visual imagery. The final drawing is laminated, with one copy given to the executive for placement in his/her office as a daily reminder of the coaching goal and another retained by the coach for use throughout the coaching to assess progress. For examples of Visual Leadership Metaphors, see Figs. 1.1–1.3.

Frame 1
It's the external crisis of 2008-09 and the world just doesn't make sense anymore. The plan we had just won't work now. We thought we had a lot of good ideas about how to make money but everything's down the drain now.

Frame 2
I'm clearly in construction mode now. There are cranes everywhere; we're tearing down some things, and we're building up a lot of other things that will set things up well for the future.

Frame 3
I'm standing in the middle of many skyscrapers that are all aglow and working beautifully. Things are clearly robust, vibrant, and we know we can sustain this.

Drawing by Joseph Williams

Frame 1

I'm leading in the way I feel I need to lead in the situation. My effort is to connect to the people and I want to do this in a natural and intuitive way. I'm searching for the best path forward.

Frame 2

I know where I want to go. I can see the path forward.

Frame 3

I'm leading a big and efficient organization. I'm with people I like and I'm running it in a way that makes it a FUN place to be. We're making things happen without a lot of focus on who is who in the hierarchy.

Drawing by Joseph Williams

NOTE: Key Elements in these metaphors include a strong appetite for leadership, comfort with ambiguity, effective problem-solving, and collaboration between the leader and others.

Fig. 1.1 *Remarkable* leaders' metaphors

Frame 1	Frame 2	Frame 3
I'm a guide in a jungle – this is a very dense jungle with no paths at all. I have a machete that I'm using to cut the pathway through. Up over the jungle far in the distance you can see a mountain peak.	I now have more tools at my disposal – I have the machete but also a compass. But I'm still missing a map. I've made it to a camp site and the jungle is behind me. I have a guide now and we're seeking a path forward together.	I'm clearly the General now. I'm in front of a large number of troops and they're all in absolute alignment with me. I'm confident but not dictatorial. We know there are still challenges ahead.

Drawing by Joseph Williams

Frame 1	Frame 2	Frame 3
I'm a builder – it's like an urban renewal scene and I'm clearing away decay to build something strong. I can pause and I'm calm and confident about what I'm doing. I'm directing people to do what needs to be done.	I'm still building this scene – I've got the blueprints in my hand and the materials have been ordered and are being delivered so this new house can be built. You can see the frame of the house now and there's a lot of construction and other activity going on to complete this great new structure.	The house is built and the whole area has been revived – you can see little shops and activity going on all around the house. With this building site completed, we've become leaders in our industry because we've done things with this building that have never been done before.

Drawing by Joseph Williams

NOTE: Key elements in these metaphors include uncertainty, progress, confidence, enthusiasm for possibility, and distinctive results. While these are strong leadership images, their owners never quite achieved their respective Frame 3s.

Fig. 1.2 *Perilous* leaders' metaphors

In the analysis of coaching case notes, two factors were key in arriving at the identification of the aforementioned leadership types. These factors were (1) the executive's intention to learn/change behavior and (2) corroborated information from the executive's boss and HR partner about the executive's learning/behavior change.

Generally speaking, *Remarkable* leaders had strong purity of intention about learning and stretching to become even more effective than they

Frame 1	Frame 2	Frame 3
I am enjoying my work but what is lacking is freedom. The consequences of me not working essentially all the feasible hours I can is significant enough to where I would never reduce my hours. Currently, I am compensating for all the managers here.	Everything remains the same but I have some time for myself. Managers are relishing my input and are looking for opportunities to obtain it – rather than fighting or ignoring it.	Everything remains the same except I have significant freedom regarding how I use my time. This means that I can choose to work when I want to. This also means there are people who can compensate for my lack of availability.

Drawing by Joseph Williams

Frame 1	Frame 2	Frame 3
Man in the ocean just flailing away...	Same man who's now learning to swim...	This man is now Captain of a ship in the ocean. Things are calmer.

Drawing by Jeff Cain

NOTE: These images reflect leaders who are more focused on their personal leadership challenge than on the enterprises and the people whom they are leading.

Fig. 1.3 *Toxic* leaders' metaphors

already were, and this was corroborated by their bosses and HR partners. They also advanced in their careers.

Perilous leaders could be less intentional about learning and change. Often, they experienced the suggestion of their participation in a developmental activity (such as coaching) as an indictment of their capabilities rather than as an opportunity for growth and development. In other words, the suggestion of coaching was a narcissistic injury for some.[12] Little will happen if this barrier is not eliminated in the coaching relationship. When it is, at least a modicum of progress is possible, and even career progress can occur.

The *Toxic* leaders in this sample date back to the 1980s when I coached such individuals. I do not do so currently because it can be a significant waste of company resources and of the time of both executive and coach.[13] Further, in my experience, *Toxic* leaders who agree to participate in coaching when suggested by a boss or senior HR professional often do so only because it would "look bad" if they did not. This constitutes a charade in which no one wins – and coaching as a valuable development tool gets sullied in the minds of company sponsors who are expecting to see a positive ROI. Further, many *Toxic* leaders really require a clinical intervention (e.g., individual psychotherapy, marital therapy, treatment for substance abuse, etc.), not coaching. Still others, who are incompetent in their roles, need that truth telling from their bosses and a role change or dismissal from the company if there is not a role in which they can succeed.

In summary, the more employees and leaders alike understand about the *how* of leadership, the better they will negotiate and thrive in this era of intense behavioral scrutiny of leaders. The following chapters provide a deeper understanding of *Remarkable*, *Perilous*, and *Toxic* leaders. It is my hope that this material is both memorable and instructive.

End Notes

[1]   Empathy in this context involves leaders' abilities to put themselves in the shoes of others and to appreciate fully and without defensiveness the perspectives, questions, and/or concerns of others – and to be appropriately responsive to them.

[2]   One excellent example of this is using questions derived from the dimensions of emotional intelligence as a tool to screen more aggressively for the "behavior fit" of prospective managers (Wasylyshyn 2010).

[3]   My executive coaching model consists of four distinct phases that typically unfold over 12–15 months. These phases are (1) data gathering, (2) feedback, (3) coaching, and (4) consolidation. After the coaching engagement is completed, many executives retain me as a *trusted advisor* on issues related to people management, their continued evolution as leaders, and CEO succession. These relationships often continue for several years, allowing me to track their careers.

[4]   Erikson is among life stage development theorists to include Anna Freud, Margaret Mahler, Mary Ainsworth, and Carl Jung. Other life

stage theorists focusing primarily on the adult life stages include Daniel Levinson and Howard Gardner.

5 *State* assessment tools provide information that is reflective of the test taker's current state of mind. If the same person took the same test some months or years later, there could be changes in the results – based on new learning or life experiences. *Trait* assessment tools provide information about enduring behavioral preferences that are unlikely to change, i.e., they remain stable over time.

6 NEO-PI-R subscales: for Neuroticism (N) = anxiety, angry hostility, depression, self-consciousness, impulsiveness, and vulnerability; for Extraversion (E) = warmth, gregariousness, assertiveness, activity, excitement seeking, positive emotions; for Openness (O) = fantasy, esthetics, feelings, actions, ideas, and values; for Agreeableness (A) = straightforwardness, altruism, compliance, modesty, and tender-mindedness; for Conscientiousness (C) = competence, order, dutifulness, achievement striving, self-discipline, and deliberation.

7 EQ-i subscales: for Intrapersonal = self-regard, emotional self-awareness, assertiveness, independence, and self-actualization; for Interpersonal = empathy, social responsibility, and interpersonal relationship; for Stress Management = stress tolerance and impulse control; for Adaptability = reality testing, flexibility, and problem-solving; for General Mood = optimism and happiness.

8 In the practice of 360 data gathering, typically an internal or external consultant speaks to a representative group of people in a leader's work sphere – boss, peers, direct reports, other key stakeholders, and if appropriate, certain external sources (e.g., board member, a major customer). These conversations usually occur face-to-face or telephonically and are based on an interview protocol that consists of questions focused on the key leadership competencies of the organization (e.g., forming strategy, managing people, driving results) as well as essential leadership behaviors (e.g., courage, emotional fortitude, accountability, attunement to others, empathy).

9 *Strategy* – the ability to formulate, convey, and achieve strategy alignment. Ensuring implementation of strategic objectives. *Driving Results* – ensuring profitable results for the enterprise. *Managing People* – ensuring the right people in the right roles, creating the conditions for them to be successful, and leveraging all motivational tools to ensure sustained commitment of the workforce. *Executive Credibility* – integrity, strong ethical code, and command skills to include courage, consistency, and persuasive, authentic communication skills.

[10] The acronym SO SMART® was created to help clients recall the four dimensions of emotional intelligence – SO for self-observation, SM for self-management, A for attunement to others, and RT for relationship traction, i.e., relationships that are meaningful, not just transitional.

[11] I created this tool to help concretize the stages of a coaching engagement and to track progress. In the ideal, a client should have made full progress in coaching, i.e., achieved the behavioral goal captured in Frame 3 of his/her Visual Leadership Metaphor.

[12] In the late 1970s and early 1980s when executive coaching emerged as a development tool, it was most often used for derailing or otherwise remedial indications. In the last decade, the emphasis has shifted toward using coaching for top high-potential people – people who would bring a positive learning attitude to the experience. A better spend on development resources, coaching ROI research has begun to show the benefit of reserving this resource for true high-potential employees (Braddick and Braddick 2003).

[13] Potential coaching engagements need to be evaluated carefully, i.e., coach of prospective client and prospective client meet to ensure that executive coaching is the right development tool and that the chemistry between client and coach is positive.

The *Remarkable* Business Leader

2

Leadership is fundamentally about one thing: connecting two points in the longest distance in the world – the one between the head and the heart.

Brian Concannon
CEO, Haemonetics

Matthew was among the brightest corporate executives in this global pharmaceutical company. His technical background and business acumen were unparalleled. He inspired confidence inside the company as well as with Wall Street analysts and investors. As a leader, he pursued an aggressive strategic agenda evoking an odd combination of awe and fear from the people who reported to him.

Soon after receiving a major promotion, he requested and received a comprehensive 360 feedback. The results were a stunning condemnation of his leadership style. He learned that his brilliance, intensity, and micromanagement had had serious disempowering and de-motivating effects on his direct reports. In an off-site retreat with his leadership team, he courageously apologized, expressed his regret, made no excuses, and committed to a number of changes in his leadership behavior.

Eighteen months later, having delivered on his behavioral change agenda, he had attained the committed dedication of his leadership team members. He had deepened his relationships with other key stakeholders. He had accelerated business results. He had orchestrated the emergence of a truly empowered and high-performing team. While he remained mindful of the possibility that he could regress to old behaviors under stress, his heightened commitment to managing his stress kept that likelihood at bay.

As we explore what makes leaders *Remarkable*, we are looking at this information primarily through the lens of how it informs ways to manage them more effectively. The specifics of this boss management are discussed in Chap. 6. Further, if you are a leader now, this information can enrich or test what you already know about effective leadership. If you aspire to become a *Remarkable* leader, consider this information as giving you a running start toward achieving that aspiration.

Life History

The *Remarkable* leaders in this sample shared a number of life history factors. These included (1) a two-parent family, (2) at least a college education, (3) marriage and a <5% divorce rate, (4) at least two children, (5) discovery of their life's work before reaching age 30, and (6) steady career histories (fewer than three company changes).

In general, they moved through Erikson's eight life stages smoothly, i.e., they were on time in accomplishing the developmental task associated with each life stage. Beginning with Stage 1 (birth-1 year), their physical and emotional needs were met; therefore, there was a strong likelihood of their forming trusting relationships later in life.

The Stage 2 (ages 1–3) task of exploring and becoming increasingly independent was assured completion by parents who were neither over-controlling or absent. By age three or four, *Remarkables* were showing Stage 3 (ages 3–5) signs of goal-oriented behavior to the delight and tireless encouragement of their parents and other caregivers. Given the attentiveness of their parents and babysitters, it was not uncommon for them to know the alphabet, numbers to 100, and to already be reading by the time they entered first grade.

Early in primary school, they displayed a Stage 4 (ages 6–11) belief in their ability to learn, solve simple problems, and accomplish goals they had set for themselves (e.g., doing well in school, making things with building toys, cooking simple recipes, etc.). These accomplishments contributed mightily to their can-do attitudes and growing sense of confidence. Many had received early messages from family members and/or teachers about their potential to excel. Those who did not receive these messages, tended to self-ignite through the discovery of things they were passionate about such as a hobby, school subject, or athletic skill. For some, their self-ignited confidence combined with a strong desire to "show" others what they could achieve. This was a fire that would burn throughout their lives.

By Stage 5 (ages 12–18), most *Remarkable* leaders had met the identity task and displayed early leadership behavior through such activities as scouting, special interest clubs, class officer roles, and sports teams. They had also begun to identify areas for further study that would ultimately influence important career decisions. While most had the advantage of a parent or teacher guiding their college decisions, others fended well for themselves making choices that were driven by their scholastic strengths, geographic preferences, college reputation/status, and budding career inclinations.

While *Remarkable* leaders had their share of adolescent growing pains and social disappointments, for the most part they were sufficiently resilient and focused to move through the developmental hurdles of Stage 6 (ages 18–35) well. They discovered and pursued a course of study that resulted in successful and rewarding careers. Over 50% of them pursued graduate study in business, law, and/or the sciences. By their early 30s, all had married and started their families.

In many respects, the accomplishments of Stage 6 set the stage well for the easier unfolding of Stage 7 (ages 35–55). Given the good decisions they had made professionally and their accumulated successes, most were eager and ready to impart knowledge and experiences to others, thus meeting the developmental challenge of generativity. For many, this meant a more intentional focus on mentoring talented high-potential employees in their organizations. For others, this meant assuming leadership roles in community-based charitable organizations. For some, it was a combination of both internal mentoring and externally focused volunteerism. Every *Remarkable* leader in this sample was committed to grooming people who could potentially succeed him/her. They also ensured a focus on talent management generally in their organizations.

The one issue that Stage 7 *Remarkables* grappled with less effectively was what is commonly referred to as work–family balance (I prefer the term work–family integration).[1] The demands on their time increase exponentially as they move toward C-level roles, and the necessity of travel – especially if they are doing business on a global scale – poses a relentless drain on quality time for family members. While there are no easy solutions, every executive family is well-served by making this a priority, i.e., an issue that gets discussed openly and one for which they find their own coping techniques – and rewards.

By the time *Remarkable* leaders hit Stage 8 (ages 55-death), they are in a sound state of mental preparedness for "the rest of the journey," as one of my CEO clients once described it. Having performed admirably professionally, groomed others well, maintained strong family and other personal relationships, and even cultivated a compelling non-work interest or two, they had a highly integrated and contented sense of themselves and the life they'd lead. Steady feelings of satisfaction, peace, and calm dominated as they began planning for their life-after-work transition.

This is not to say that these transitions are necessarily smooth. They are not because they involve a destruction of what *was* and the creation of a new life model. While most *Remarkables* (who reached retirement at this writing) were sufficiently planful and had supportive marital partners who were pleased to "get them back," others struggled for they had not been as planful as they needed to be. These leaders found my *Five P Model for Career After Life* helpful.[2]

Psychological Testing Results

Overall, *Remarkable* leaders did extraordinarily well on each of the five psychometric tools described in Chap. 1. Based on the Watson–Glaser Critical Thinking Appraisal, they fall into the superior–very superior ranges when compared to executive and manager norm groups. This finding indicates that their abilities to study a body of facts, arrive at logical conclusions, and set sound priorities are very highly evolved. Obviously, these are critical abilities in senior leadership roles.

On a measure of behavior preferences, The Myers–Briggs Type Indicator, most of these leaders were at least moderately extraverted, intuitive, relied on objective data for decision-making, and were quick to judge mediocre performance. Most had a preference for order and thoroughness; however, they were also comfortable with ambiguity. Behaviorally, they tend to be direct and decisive. They take a systematic approach to problem-solving and strive to maintain traction and momentum on identified goals. They will be sensitive to people and organizational dynamics, but they are not going to be distracted by them. They prefer multi-talented teams that include members who compensate for their own weaknesses. While they prize and seek innovative ideas, they require sufficient objective data before investing considerable resources in them.

Based on the Life Styles Inventory (LSI), *Remarkables* consistently tested as having constructive thinking styles. This means they are likely to be excellent leaders because they are focused on (1) joint achievements; (2) the self-actualization of themselves and others, i.e., ensuring that one becomes all that he/she is capable of becoming; (3) providing humanistic and committed support for the growth and development of others; and (4) forming relationships through which the work evolves and people thrive in authentic and caring relationships with each other.

Remarkable leaders proved to be psychologically fit and robust on the NEO-PI-R, a measure based on the Big 5 Factor theory of personality explained in Chap. 1. To summarize, they were (1) resilient versus neurotic, (2) extraverted, (3) open, (4) moderately agreeable (their intellectual discernment moderated this factor), and (5) highly conscientious.

The NEO-PI-R was one of the psychological assessment tools used in the empirical research described in Chap. 1. To recap, compared to *Perilous* and *Toxic* leaders, *Remarkable* leaders were found to be more (1) resilient than neurotic, (2) extraverted (gregarious), (3) conscientious (belief in their abilities, working efficiently, adherence to ethical and moral obligations, focused and discipline), and (4) assertive. Based on this data, it also appears that *Remarkable* leaders prefer a faster pace than *Perilous* and *Toxic* leaders.

The Emotional Quotient Inventory (EQ-i) was the other psychological assessment tool used in the empirical research described in Chap. 1. In a nutshell, *Remarkable* leaders possess strong emotional intelligence. As described in Chap. 1, the four core dimensions of emotional intelligence are represented by the acronym SO SMART (Wasylyshyn 2003).[3]

Starting with the foundational dimension of self-observation, they possess an accurate understanding of their own strengths and weaknesses. They strive to leverage their strengths and to minimize any adverse effects or weaknesses by remaining self-aware, seeking and using frequent feedback, and surrounding themselves with people who fill their gaps. Through an accurate perception of their own and others' emotions, they bring another powerful resource to the act of leading well. Specifically, they can rely on their emotions – along with objective thoughts – to inform sound, even stellar, leadership behavior.

Able to control and channel their emotions – both positive (e.g., happiness, anticipation, excitement, pride in work well done) and negative (e.g., anger, disappointment, frustration, apprehension) – *Remarkable* leaders can use their emotional awareness often with stunning results. For example, they can sound the inspirational clarion call to motivate others and they can also deliver the tough – albeit constructive messages – necessary for change.

A CEO of a global manufacturing company once described this as "passion with a deadline." Embedded in this comment are both the urgency for action and the positive emotion essential to drive results. These leaders are also characterized by their extraordinary resilience – both in good times and especially in the face of adversity.

Their attunement to others distinguishes *Remarkable* leaders both inside and outside their organizations. They possess an uncanny ability to use their emotions to see what they need to see and to hear what they need to hear. This attunement is natural and reflexive whether they are interacting at the board level, within their leadership teams, with employees in other geographical regions, or with critical external stakeholders. Their focus on others is at once genuine and piercing in a manner that helps forge lasting trust. Because *Remarkable* leaders strive to have an empathic understanding of others' concerns, anxieties, and aspirations, they build deep commitment and loyalty. Equally important, such attunement enables them to accrue "grace points" that are banked and drawn upon when things go awry.

Because *Remarkable* leaders strive to understand the emotional states of others, they are able to form authentic and lasting connections. In the workplace, their relationships are not merely transactional (*I need you to do this now*). Instead, these leaders establish meaningful connections with others and have knowledge of their personal lives. This has obvious implications for their ability to ensure the commitment of high-performing teams that are distinguished by goal-oriented collaboration and often breakthrough results.

Core Leadership Competencies

The success of *Remarkable* leaders like Matthew is distinguished by the strength of the four leadership competencies described in Chap. 1 (1) strategy, (2) driving results, (3) managing people, and (4) executive credibility. *Remarkable* leaders are not only strong in each of these competencies – they are gifted in the ability to leverage the interaction among them. When/ if they consider themselves less effective in any of these competency areas, they are likely to import the necessary talent to their leadership teams rather than risk a continuing competency deficit. These competencies are defined in Table 2.1.

Since they are also solid in the four dimensions of emotional intelligence (as described above under Psychological Testing Results), like Matthew, they exemplify *total brain leadership* (*TBL*) – the integration of left brain (IQ) and right brain (EQ) functioning. This integration can enrich both the quality of their decision-making and their relationships inside and outside their companies (Wasylyshyn 2003). The importance of this integration of left and right brain functioning cannot be overstated in that many business leaders are overdeveloped in one dimension – the cognitive.

As Kaplan and Kaiser (2003) noted, "Leadership consists of opposing strengths, and most leaders have a natural tendency to overdevelop one at the expense of its counterpart. This resulting imbalance diminishes their effectiveness" (p. 19).

It's no accident that business leaders can over-rely on a particular strength like analytical problem-solving, for example. This strength surely works; it's

Table 2.1 Four leadership competencies

Strategy	Sees ahead clearly; can anticipate future consequences and trends accurately; has broad knowledge and perspective; is future oriented; can paint credible pictures and visions of possibilities and likelihoods; can create competitive and breakthrough strategies and plans
Driving results	Can be counted on to exceed goals successfully; is constantly and consistently one of the top performers; very bottom-line oriented; steadfastly pushes self and others for results
Managing people	Ensuring clarity about roles, responsibilities, resources and direction. Achieving alignment on objectives, as well as efficient and cost effective results. Providing frequent and candid performance feedback. Remaining focused on people's ongoing needs for learning and development
Executive credibility	Possessing strong character, integrity, and ethical principles. Communicating with clarity and confidence in the future. Behaving consistently and with the courage of one's convictions

reliable, and it's a core factor in executives being rewarded well. But over-reliance on a strength – when a broader array of capabilities is required to be fully effective – can be a serious problem. This is as true in professional sports as it is in business. Consider Andy Roddick who arguably has one of the best serves in men's tennis and yet he's not won a major tournament in several years given his failure to lift the rest of his game – especially the mental part of it – to the level of that astounding serve.

Kaplan and Kaiser (2003) suggest that the key to executives moderating overused strengths is for them to place less value on them, to identify less with a particular strength, and to ease up on the use of them. In their words, "The key to moderating strengths that have been taken to an extreme is for managers to learn to be more nuanced in their application… they need to see the control mechanism not as an on-off switch, but rather as a dial, one that they can simply turn down a notch or two. They don't have to give up their gift; they can instead make more discriminating, and therefore more effective, use of it" (p. 25).

This is good advice – especially if followed in concert with an intentional stretch toward releasing[4] other capabilities that would enable them to lead with a more balanced mix of leadership strengths.

Strategy

Their effectiveness in formulating strategy is supported by a number of distinctive abilities. These include (1) superior analytical abilities (as measured by the Watson–Glaser), (2) rapid recognition of business patterns, (3) accurate synthesis of their own and others' thoughts about these patterns, and (4) the ability to articulate a clear, compelling and inspirational picture of the future.

Remarkable leaders also understand the power of inclusion and prefer that all key people are at the table when strategy is formulated. In their subsequent ambassadorial roles, direct reports along with the leader, ensure strategic alignment and execution. McKnight, Kaney and Breuer (2010) emphasize, "No strategy can succeed if the people who have to implement it don't understand it. If kept in the dark, employees are but passengers along for the ride. Having said this, it's astonishing how few executives make sure that employees understand the business, how it works, the factors critical for winning or, indeed, the strategy itself" (p. 43).

Finally, *Remarkable* leaders have a "nose" for unexpected flaws in a strategy and for recognizing early warning signs that necessitate rapid adjustments. Their agile thinking and cognitive flexibility are other differentiating factors among these leaders because their egos don't get in the way with defensive reasoning or other immature behaviors (Argyris 1991).

Driving Results

Early in their careers, *Remarkable* leaders learn to make a strong distinction between activity and results. They have a special radar for seeing when people have busied themselves with activities that are not critical to reaching identified objectives. They also have the courage to call out this behavior and get people refocused. They understand the continuing nature of gauging clarity and of ensuring it along with encouragement and sufficient resources so objectives are met. At the same time, they expect sustained momentum and will not be patient with excuses, missed deadlines, or anything else that deters expected outcomes. Former Rohm and Haas (now DOW) executives referred to this essential leadership behavior as "steel trap accountability."[5]

Managing People

Remarkable leaders know that even the best strategies will not ensure business success if they don't have talented people in key roles and an organization structure that supports strategic priorities. They lead by the axiom that structure follows strategy. These leaders also understand that their jobs are easier when they have ensured the right conditions for people to be successful. This begins with role clarity and everyone understanding his/her core responsibilities, as well as how things are to be achieved – technically, managerially, and behaviorally.

Remarkable leaders are also intentional about giving feedback – frequent, specific, and constructive performance feedback that reinforces what people are doing right and instructs on how they may need to do things differently. For these leaders, this is not the dreaded annual performance review; it is a dynamic and ongoing process of give-and-take that anticipates problems, unleashes mutual problem-solving, and ensures the delivery of necessary results (see the poem, "Duende" in Chap. 9 for a metaphorical representation of this type of feedback).

Executive Credibility

The executive credibility of *Remarkable* leaders is another strong suit based on the interaction of at least three factors: communication, consistency and courage. They are usually fluid and compelling communicators who are able to connect with both large and small groups effectively. They may have come by this naturally, or they may have done the necessary work with a communications expert who helped them find their own authentic way of reaching people – whether it's in the corporate Board room or at a town hall meeting in Asia.

With *Remarkable* leaders, there is enormous consistency between what they say and do. They resist both hyperbolic and passive representations of the future. They remain mindful of maintaining a realistic perspective for all stakeholders. This necessitates three things (1) truth telling about the present, (2) acknowledgement about the things in the organizations that are working and bode well for the future, and (3) bridging from the now to a hopeful picture of the future. More will be said about this leadership tool of *perspective-making* in Chap. 7.

Remarkable leaders maintain the courage of their convictions but beyond that, and perhaps more importantly, they are fearless. This is an informed courage – being bold but not reckless in the pursuit of business goals and success. They relish leading, are willing to speak out, stand alone, influence open debate, probe unexpressed views, and leverage resident wisdom. They are also willing to confront company "sacred cows," decisions, policies, and/or practices that could impede business success.

Coaching Notes

Remarkable leaders are intentional about their continuous learning – including behavioral change if that is warranted. Their HR partners typically provided corroborating information about the commitment of these leaders to their ongoing development as leaders. Their impressive career progressions stand as testimony to their learning efforts.

In coaching them, I observed an array of other admirable behaviors. These behaviors included patience, the ability to tolerate frustration, flexibility, and non-defensiveness. Like Matthew, they can "own" their mistakes, learn from them, and move on without undue self-chastisement or rumination. While they are typically ambitious, they are not preoccupied with self-image or advancement or the trappings of power. Instead, they are dedicated to serving their organizations capably by ensuring business results, modeling enterprise thinking and behavior, and developing a bench of talented employees who continue to learn and evolve technically and/or managerially.

Given their preference for trusting in the capabilities and intentions of others, *Remarkable* leaders readily form high-impact teams. Members of their teams feel empowered and well-motivated by shared goals and group cohesion. The deep sense of satisfaction that *Remarkable* leaders typically take from their work cascades over their teams influencing collective feelings of meaning – and even fun.

Remarkable leaders are typically open to new learning, can tolerate ambiguity, and can assume the perspective of another. While certain single-minded, super confident, and powerful *Remarkable* leaders could be described as narcissistic, they are what Maccoby (2000) described as "productive narcissists." Current business leaders to include Bill Gates (Microsoft); Steve Jobs (Apple); former eBay CEO, Meg Whitman; FMC Chairman and CEO, Pierre Brondeau; and DuPont Chairman and CEO, Ellen Kullman, all personify this positive business persona. They are brilliant, confident, courageous, and relentlessly clear about their strategic pursuits, key people, and operational decisions.

On a continuum of narcissistic behavior running from productive to unproductive to malignant narcissism, the *Remarkable* leader would clearly be at the productive end of the continuum. For perspective, failed CEOs including Dennis Koslowski (TYCO), Durk Jager (Proctor & Gamble), Al "Chainsaw" Dunlap (Scott Paper and Sunbeam), Robert Nardelli (Home Depot), and Ken Lay (Enron) would fall into the unproductive range. Certain political monsters of the world to include Adolf Hitler, Idi Amin, and Osama Bin Laden would be at the malignant end of this continuum (see Fig. 2.1).

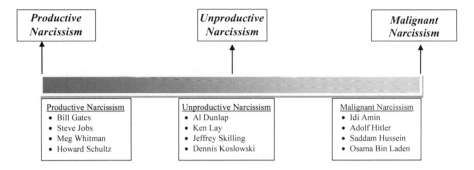

Fig. 2.1 Continuum of narcissism

In summary, there is much that readily distinguishes *Remarkable* business leaders. They are total brain leaders (TBL) possessing a distinct combination of intellectual capabilities and behavioral assets. They are strategic, results driven, excellent managers of people, and enormously credible within their companies and with critical external constituencies as well. They are also emotionally smart given their high self-awareness, discipline, empathy, and ability to form authentic relationships with diverse people on a global landscape. Finally, their healthy psyches enable them to share success and guide others – including their successors – over key development hurdles. This might just be their biggest competitive leadership edge of all.

Remarkable leaders – like Paul (see box) are often spotted early.

Paul joined the Research division of a global chemical company and did well in his early technical roles. However, what emerged fairly quickly were his distinctive abilities to identify growth prospects, engage well with his commercial peers in the company, and an overall business acumen that set him apart from his Research colleagues. His impressive combination of strategic thinking, operational strength, and people management capabilities further identified him as a top high-potential manager. Behaviorally, he was courageous, charming, confident, steady, and charismatic.

People craved to work for him and learned well under his demanding tutelage. His loyalty and commitment to them influenced their prolific efforts. He practiced the annual performance review as an art and focused relentlessly on getting the right people in the right roles and creating the right conditions for them to be successful (see *Duende* in Chap. 9). A relentless work-hard-play-hard leader, members of his teams learned the incalculable importance of fun.

As he helped propel the company's presence in Asia and build a new business platform that contributed exponentially to the growth of the company, his name was an obvious one for the CEO succession list. Well-mentored by the sitting CEO, when he was made President, the succession appeared set – until the company was acquired by a giant other in their space.

Unable to work in the culture of the acquiring company – despite the senior role he was given – he resigned and soon found himself with a number of attractive roles to consider. Ultimately, he accepted a CEO role in another global company that had been led by a brilliant, operations-oriented executive. The mission here would be growth – and the opportunity to change a command and control alpha culture. Paul's experience, combination of left and right brain capabilities, interpersonal gifts, resilience, and fundamental belief in the power of team-based leadership would serve him, the employees, and the shareholders well.

The *Remarkable* Leader

	Ratings		
	Strong	Variable	Weak
I – Leadership competencies			
A. Strategy	✓		
B. Drives results	✓		
C. People	✓		
D. Executive credibility	✓		
II – Emotional intelligence (SO SMART)			
A. Self observation	✓		
B. Self management	✓		
C. Attunement	✓		
D. Relationship traction	✓		

End Notes

[1]   The author uses the more apt term "work–family integration" instead of the popular "work–family balance" terminology. For top talent individuals, work–family balance – if considered literally as a balance between

the two domains of work and family – is an impossible objective to achieve. On the other hand, everyone should strive to find her/his version of work–family integration.

2   The five P Model for Career After Life is a holistic planning process that focuses on five essential factors (1) Purpose (identification of activities that will give one's life meaning), (2) People (identification of the people one most wants to spend time with), (3) Place (making decisions regarding where one most wants to live and in what type of dwelling), (4) Physical (promoting one's healthy lifestyle and physical well-being), and (5) Prosperity (deciding/planning of all financial-related issues). For some who are more spiritually oriented, there is a 6th P – "Phaith."

3   Emotional Intelligence (EQ) – the awareness of one's own and others' emotions and the ability to discriminate among them. The ability to use that emotional awareness to achieve work and personal objectives (see Table 2.1).

4   I purposely use the term *releasing* and not *developing* because in my experience with senior business leaders, they often have a strong left brain cognitive preference and appetite for facts and data but they are not without right brain conceptual and interpersonal capabilities. In other words, their lopsided leadership styles are a function of their having chosen to cultivate a certain leadership persona and/or they have been socialized to reveal and revere only certain parts of themselves. When leadership circumstances necessitate their tapping into behaviors or abilities that have been masked or otherwise diminished, they can – especially when they are encouraged and valued for doing so.

5   Steel trap accountability – relentless drive for results. No defensiveness. No sad stories. No excuses. No blaming others. Making the necessary adjustments (in people, process, and/or strategy) if needed – and doing it quickly. Hard work alone is not enough – the results have to be there.

The *Perilous* Business Leader

No disaster is worse than being discontented.

Lao Tzu
Chinese Philosopher

For the first decade of his career, Victor distinguished himself in the trade publishing industry as a stunningly creative and brilliant marketing talent. Described by one of his bosses as "scary smart," he had been the catalytic force in the launching of several successful healthcare publications. Strategic, articulate, and a superb writer, he was poised for a corporate role but certain behavior problems got in the way.

Deep-seated issues with authority figures often blocked Victor's ability to handle disagreements with senior management, and eventually he was perceived as too much of a "loose cannon." Equally strong competitive instincts that masked his considerable insecurity made him a challenging handful for peers. Given his lack of confidence in others and poor delegation skills, the people who reported to him often felt unfairly criticized and disempowered.

His personal life was littered with tumultuous relationships including two divorces. As the gap between reality and his professional and personal aspirations widened, his drinking took its toll on the quality of his work. When the publishing industry began to reel with the emergence of electronic media, Victor's opportunities diminished significantly and he could not summon the emotional resilience to "reinvent" himself. He sunk into a serious depression, gained an enormous amount of weight, suffered a third divorce, and his mourning of the days that were – of what he could have been – blocked any view of a productive path forward. This brilliant shooting star just flamed out.

The fundamental lack of contentment with the self, this sense of unrequitedness can be, as it was for Victor, a self-fulfilling prophecy for many.[1] Their feelings of "unrequited work" fester internally and can seep out or

K.M. Wasylyshyn, *Behind the Executive Door: Unexpected Lessons for Managing Your Boss and Career*, DOI 10.1007/978-1-4614-0376-0_3,
© Karol M. Wasylyshyn 2012

even explode in sudden acts of poor leadership that stun or leave those who work for them in a state of anticipatory dread. See the exercise below for a checklist of "unrequited work" factors.

Exercise

TEN INDICATORS – A SENSE ——————— OF UNREQUITED WORK ———————

Instruction: Check the following statements that apply to you.

____ I really don't enjoy work that much; I had envisioned that I would be a lot happier in my work.

____ I don't think I was meant to do this work – it just turned out that way.

____ I regret not pursuing another career direction that I had had in mind. I think I would have been more contented with my work had I done that.

____ I wish I had been more proactive in planning my career.

____ I have been envious of others who were more focused and directed about their work pursuits.

____ My work is more of a means to an end than something that is meaningful to me.

____ When I started working, I had envisioned myself going much further than I have.

____ Sometimes I think I've wasted a lot of time when it comes to work. I have not become all that I believe I could be.

____ The best thing I can say about my work is that it enabled me to meet my family and other financial responsibilities.

____ I look forward to retirement so I can do things that will give me a lot more enjoyment than I'm experiencing now.

KEY

Three checked items indicates a low sense of unrequited work. You may be more content than you think.

Four to seven checked items indicates a moderate sense of unrequited work. Consider possible changes.

Eight or more checked items indicates a high sense of unrequited work. A change is definitely warranted.

A closer look at the *Perilous* leadership is provided below based on the following data (1) life history, (2) psychological test results, (3) leadership competencies, and (4) coaching notes.

Life History

The *Perilous* leaders in this sample shared a number of life history factors. These included (1) harsh, judgmental parents whose affection for their children was conditional upon the children performing well; (2) little affirmation from parents or other caregivers; (3) a college education; (4) at least one divorce; (5) at least two children but relationships with them were often strained; (6) difficulty in settling into a career path; and (7) career histories with either just one – or several employers.[2]

Developmentally, *Perilous* leaders experienced difficulties in accomplishing the necessary psychosocial tasks of the eight Eriksonian stages. While there were no Stage 1 (birth-1 year) issues in terms of basic physical needs being met, they did not, for the most part, receive the consistent affection and emotional nurturance as did *Remarkable* leaders. The mothers of some – like Marvin described in Chap. 1 – experienced varying degrees of postpartum depression. Other mothers, fathers, and/or additional care givers were emotionally ill-equipped to be as responsive as the infant needed them to be. Herein were the seeds of mistrust that would try all future relationships.

In Stage 2 (ages 1–3), their beginning independent actions might have been encouraged, but it was not without the critical judging and/or controlling behavior of their parents. Thus, early feelings of shame or doubt began to be internalized.

For the most part, the preschool or nursery school years of *Perilous* leaders were characterized by increasing goal-oriented behavior like braver explorations of the world around them and freer expressions and questions about what they were seeing. While such behavior is indicative of Stage 3 (ages 3–5) initiative, for many this came with the psychological price of their parents' displeasure or punishment. This behavior on the part of parents or other caregivers catalyzed the child's earliest feelings of guilt – with lifelong effects.

By Stage 4 (ages 6–11), things began to get more complicated developmentally for *Perilous* leaders. Most became aware of their own brain power and the concomitant confidence that they could rely on this for achievement. Generally, these leaders performed well in primary school – for most were still striving to meet their parents' expectations and receive indications of approval. However, some of these leaders were so smart, they were bored and disengaged. Others floundered in school because their parents were too absent to recognize their child's learning struggle. And still others were already displaying behavioral problems – like acting out – that interfered with a successful primary education. However, most of these children surmounted their early learning and/or behavioral difficulties to commence careers in which they at least did well financially.

Developmental complications continued for many *Perilous* leaders in Stage 5 (ages 12–18). The psychological wounds from previous development stages interfered with or blocked achievement of the Stage 5 task of forming a strong sense of identity. Most would describe themselves as having "muddled through" and accidentally winding up in a good college and on the path toward a satisfying and productive life – despite their inner demons.[3] Others would tell a different story – a story characterized by the lifelong theme of never quite becoming what they wanted to be – what they could have been.

The Stage 6 (ages 18–35) task of intimacy, i.e., settling into/becoming intimate with (1) a consistent work pursuit and (2) a primary love relationship with another person posed different challenges for *Perilous* leaders. Many simply happened into their careers and eventually found at least some contentment within them. And the same was true of their personal lives characterized by an "OK" first marriage and then a better choice second time around. There were some who found an ideal first marital partner; however, their full happiness and intimacy in these relationships appeared to be diminished by chronic discontent regarding work.

The generativity task of Stage 7 (ages 35–55) was inevitably more difficult for *Perilous* leaders. There was not enough self-affirmation, pleasure, and passion about their work pursuits to fuel their desire to guide the next generation. There was too much psychological clutter, waste, and mental cacophony for them to clearly see their accomplishments and how this information could help teach, prepare, and inform others. Some of these leaders were too embittered to become engaged in such efforts. But there were others who got through this stage well because they made enough peace with their disappointments and self-limiting thoughts to release psychic resources for promoting the growth of others.

Perhaps no development period poses as much danger to *Perilous* leaders than Stage 8 (age 55–death). This is the final psychological hurdle between happiness and despair. Will they be able to transcend the abyss of their self-created unrequitedness? Will they, like Victor, sink into a muddy rumination and boozy rendition of missed opportunities and unfair treatment? Or, will they be able to integrate all of their life experiences into one colorful – albeit patchwork – and silken life guilt? Will they be able to pull this quilt over themselves and sleep a peaceful and calmer night? For

Perilous leaders to escape the dangers of this life stage, they must replace *what might have been* with *what is* – their own human history of success and loss.

Psychological Testing Results

There were notable differences in the psychological assessment results between *Remarkable* and *Perilous* leaders. On the Watson–Glaser Critical Thinking Appraisal, *Perilous* leaders scored in the superior–very superior ranges as did *Remarkable* leaders. However, given their underlying psychological issues related to confidence and assertiveness, many of these leaders were not able to consistently apply the force of their analytical thinking strengths. There could be situational factors such as their feeling unduly scrutinized by a boss or peers that eroded their effectiveness or in some way diminished the quality of their problem-solving.

In terms of their behavior preferences, as measured by the Myers–Briggs Type Indicator, the great majority of *Perilous* leaders tested as introverts who prefer a pragmatic focus on achieving current objectives and who rely primarily on objective data for decision-making. Some *Perilous* leaders have a strong preference for clarity and well-thought-out plans, while others are quite comfortable with ambiguity and may lack an orderly and disciplined approach. Because they tend to be more quiet, reserved, or even detached, concerted efforts need to be made by others to ascertain what they are really thinking because they are usually thinking at a fairly deep level. Invariably, they will jump to problem-solving before they have grasped inherent people issues that warrant equal attention. Given the independent nature of their thinking, they are not always the most inclusive and empowering of leaders.

Regarding how their thinking influences their behavior as managers of people, the picture as presented by the Life Styles Inventory (LSI) was also mixed. The clearest favorable theme – when comparing *Perilous* leaders to the *Remarkable* – was their strong achievement orientation. In a less favorable light, *Perilous* leaders showed elevations in competitive and perfectionistic dimensions – not surprising in the context of their upbringings.

Perilous leaders also presented variable results on the NEO-PI-R, a measure based on the Big 5 Factor Theory of personality and one of the ones used in the empirical research discussed in Chap. 1. When compared to *Remarkable* leaders, the clearest themes were (1) less resilience under pressure/stress, (2) less gregarious, (3) less likely to work without distraction, (4) less straightforward, and (5) less modest, i.e., more preoccupied with themselves and their needs.

On the Emotional Quotient Inventory (EQ-i), another psychological assessment tool used in the empirical research described in Chap. 1, *Perilous* leaders were found to be less emotionally intelligent than *Remarkable* leaders but generally more so than *Toxic* leaders. While there were some notable exceptions in this sample, i.e., executives who scored in the above average range, for the most part, these EQ scores were in the average or below average ranges.

Compared to *Remarkable* leaders, they were not as self-aware and therefore had a less accurate picture of their strengths and weaknesses. They usually did not manage their emotions consistently well – especially negative emotion as related to their frustration and disappointments in the performance of others. Regarding positive emotion, they were parsimonious in their recognition of others' efforts and results.

Given their self-preoccupation, *Perilous* leaders were not as attuned to the needs and concerns of others. Since their ability to display empathy was limited, they could not use this as a vehicle for resonance with others nor could they benefit from its motivational effects. Their relationships tended to be more transactional than meaningful on a personal level. This is not to say that these leaders could not "turn on the charm" – they certainly did but this was often more manipulative and opportunistic than authentic.

Interpersonally, *Perilous* leaders could be masterful chameleons engaging others intently – especially key stakeholders such as the boss, board members, or customers. However, their relationships with direct reports were rarely close – unless someone was serving a very specific purpose. For example, one leader had a pattern of playing "good cop, bad cop" with his Human Resources (HR) Director who always assumed the "bad cop" role. While this was a partnership that kept the boss away from personnel "dirty work," over time serious trust issues were aroused in the organization that ultimately destroyed the credibility of the HR professional and eroded respect for the *Perilous* leader.

Their relationships with peers were particularly problematic especially when *Perilous* leaders felt challenged or threatened by others. Publicly they could appear collaborative, but behind-the-scenes, they were passive-aggressive, overtly contentious, or otherwise sabotaged their colleagues' efforts. They could also be hypervigilant about resources afforded peers and/or acknowledgements others received from senior management. At their worst, they were wracked with feelings of envy, suspiciousness, and entitlement that compromised their ability to work collegially with peers. Further, given their transactional orientation to others, *Perilous* leaders often failed to accrue the "grace points" necessary to ease tensions and disagreements.

In summary, for *Perilous* leaders, emotional intelligence was generally not a significant resource upon which they could draw for enlightened and/or empowering leadership.

Core Leadership Competencies

Based on four core leadership competencies – Strategy, Driving Results, Managing People, and Executive Credibility – *Perilous* leaders presented a "mixed" picture. In other words, they were strong on some but limited on others – especially as related to strategic clarity and people management.

Strategy

Perilous leaders were either superb or terrible with strategy – despite their innate brilliance. Certain behaviors including a preference for keeping their options open, trusting their own analyses more than those of others, and even some penchant for making chaos compromised their full effectiveness in this competency area.

These leaders could be more competitive than collaborative, or so fiercely independent that strategic decision-making got delayed beyond a reasonable timeframe. Any one of these behaviors posed a barrier to achieving rapid strategic alignment. Any combination of these behaviors influenced serious problems in the execution of core strategic objectives.

When people resisted or otherwise did not get in rapid alignment with their strategic direction, *Perilous* leaders often lacked the savoir faire to probe the source of resistance or failure to align. Instead, some became impatient and overly directive. Others became petulant – withdrawing and stewing privately in their frustration. Some leaders even capitulated to their teams' strategic preferences which may or may not have made sense depending on the quality and incisiveness of others' strategic analyses.

Driving Results

While *Perilous* leaders often drove excellent – even breakthrough – results, there could be unnecessary costs given *how* they lead. Because they were rarely satisfied, could flip flop on direction and plans, gave erratic performance feedback, and were prone to sudden bursts of anger, their teams were often emotionally fatigued, fractured, and/or dispirited.

Because they were often not the best communicators, their teams struggled with issues like role clarity, specifics regarding accountability, ambiguity about deadlines, and uncertainty about resources in terms what was or was not forthcoming.

Further, *Perilous* leaders' preoccupations with themselves and getting their own needs met sometimes interfered with their having an adequate focus on the development of talented others in their organizations. Their self-centeredness and failure to advocate for or give visibility to their people made the retention of top talent a real issue – an issue that further jeopardized the steady flow of timely and high-quality results.

Managing People

While their penchant for last-minute heroics could drive impressive business results, this behavior also disempowered and demoralized the people reporting to them. Further, they were not nearly as talented as *Remarkable* leaders in forming and maintaining high-performing teams. Their decisions in terms of ensuring that they had the best people in the right roles were often questionable. And while the direct reports of *Perilous* leaders were generally respectful of their bosses' brilliance and business acumen, they grew restless and disengaged because they did not feel well lead. They also did not believe the boss would advocate for their advancement.

High-potential employees, in particular, wearied of leaders who praised and rewarded direct reports one week and suddenly abandoned them the next. With *Perilous* leaders, things were never quite steady, and untold hours of productivity were lost as employees suffered in silence or commiserated about the leader's chronic unpredictability, insults, or lack of clarity.

Despite their strengths, working for *Perilous* leaders could be a dangerous tinder box situation. Their deeply held feelings of unrequited work could ignite unexpectedly setting off inexplicable whip-lashing behavior that confused, angered, or even hurt those around them including administrative personnel. Despite their good results – and whether *Perilous* leaders realized it or not – they could be in jeopardy of losing their jobs because their leadership behavior departed too significantly from culture norms, eroded productivity, and sabotaged the potential of high-performing teams.

Executive Credibility

Perilous leaders represented distinct plusses and minuses on the leadership competency of executive credibility. On the positive side, their innate intelligence and business acumen influenced highly credible and influential communication. Even if they were not the most gifted orators, with the help of coaching in this realm, they could be quite effective especially if they tuned into their audiences and connected with them well.

They scored less well on consistency. Given their unrequited work dynamic, they could swing behaviorally between confidence and uncertainty, optimism and pessimism. When feeling uncertain or pessimistic – or surely when they were feeling both – anger, frustration, and impatience ruled. These negative behaviors dominated what was otherwise mature, steady, and appropriate leadership behavior. *Perilous* leaders could suddenly contradict their earlier directions, look to blame others for negative outcomes, evade culpability on mistakes, and were just not as *present* as they needed to be in a crisis or otherwise threatening business situation.

The likelihood of *Perilous* leaders behaving courageously was also variable. In the presence of strong business results and high approval ratings from the stakeholders who mattered most to them (e.g., boss, board members, customers), these leaders – like many – were comfortable taking courageous stands on business issues. However, when the business climate was dire and the executive was feeling tested in ways that were threatening or otherwise ego-bruising, courageous stands on business, people, or company policy issues could be compromised.

Coaching Notes

In my experience, *Perilous* leaders were either fantastic or mediocre coaching clients.

Which way it went pivoted most on whether or not they were "hooked" into believing there was important leader development work for them to do and that absent their doing that work, they would not be as effective as they desired to be. To be more specific, without their intentional efforts to change certain self-limiting behaviors, they would not move toward *Remarkable* on the *Remarkable, Perilous, Toxic* leader behavior continuum (see Fig. 3.1). Instead, they would remain more *Perilous* than not or worse, in the presence of bad business results, they would tilt into *Toxic*. Sadly, either of these two outcomes would serve to reinforce their underlying sense of unrequitedness thus leaving them vulnerable for a late life depression.

While a strong Human Resources (HR) partner can be an ally in introducing a *Perilous* leader to the potential value of executive coaching, in the end, it is the true "readiness" of the executive to learn and to adjust behavior that will most influence a positive outcome. Such outcomes can include career advancement – assuming the leader has learned well, is committed to new behavior, avoids total behavioral regression, and can acknowledge and adjust when mini regressions have occurred. A model of behavior change is provided in Fig. 3.2.

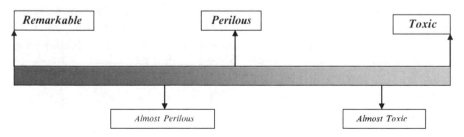

Fig. 3.1 Leadership type continuum

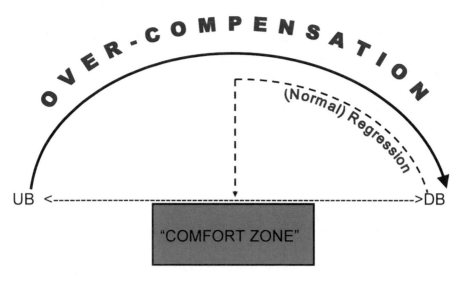

KEY

UB = UNDESIRABLE BEHAVIOR

DB = DESIRABLE BEHAVIOR

©Copyright 1992, K.M. Wasylyshyn, Psy. D., Philadelphia, PA

NOTE: Every behavior change effort involves 1) an initial phase of over-compensation that cannot be sustained (*I'm never going to eat chocolate again*), 2) some regression that is normal (*Oops, I had that piece of birthday cake*), and then 3) settling into a behavior comfort zone (*OK, so a little chocolate once in a while is OK*). The behavior change effort is successful because it can be sustained and one is not where he/she was when the change effort commenced.

Fig. 3.2 Model of behavioral change

In terms of prevalent behaviors, *Perilous* leaders were perennially dissatisfied. It didn't matter whether the issue at hand was as major as a strategy presentation or as minor as the choice of a restaurant for dinner; *Perilous* leaders were chronically disappointed. Even more frustrating is that they often feigned satisfaction in the moment – the truth of their opinions emerging only later to the dismay of others. Over time, team members were worn down or just became inured to this attitude of criticism, discontent and inconsistent behavior. Further, *Perilous* leaders did not accept negative feedback kindly. As one global Business Manager said of his boss, "Confronting him on his inconsistencies and chaos-making is nothing short of career limiting, and he'll always find a way to turn it back on me or someone else."

On the other hand, the combination of their innate strengths, leadership competencies, and modicum of emotional intelligence made them appear charming – even charismatic. Surely this is the executive persona they strove to convey. Often, they used this to recruit talented people to their organization. (See "Emperor's Jacket" in Chap. 9 as a metaphorical example of this behavior). However, unlike *Remarkable* leaders, they did not maintain this engaging behavior well. Their insecurities and underlying issues with *trust* inevitably emerged and caused relationship difficulties and/or blowups that seriously soured the work atmosphere.

Such relationship difficulties occurred at home as well as at work – although these leaders tended to do a better job at work of controlling their most divisive and hurtful behaviors. *Perilous* leaders proved to be domineering, caustic, belittling, and hypercritical in their family relationships. Their chronic feelings of discontent bled into their personal lives eroding love and intimacy in even their closest relationships. Some of these leaders whipped themselves about this behavior. Some just kept whipping the closest people around them. Some sought relief from the "noise" within by abusing alcohol or prescribed medications. Others sought escape in patterns of promiscuity that further alienated them from the possibility of intimate and consistently caring relationships with marital partners, other family members, or friends. In my experience, I have seen only a few *Perilous* leaders seek the professional help they needed to face their true selves and get recalibrated for success and trusting love relationships.

Further, *Perilous* leaders valued their work pursuits over all else. While they could project some degree of warmth, caring, and even empathy – this vanished quickly whenever someone deterred their work-related objectives. For *Perilous* leaders, their work defined them – it was the most direct expression of them. Given this degree of identity–work fusion, we must consider these leaders in the context of narcissism. Their narcissism made them even more perilous because it could be both productive and unproductive depending on the context.

In making the distinction between productive and unproductive narcissists, Maccoby (2000) wrote, "…narcissists can be extraordinarily useful – even necessary. Leaders such as Jack Welsh are productive narcissists… they are gifted and creative strategists who see the big picture and find meaning in the risky challenge of changing the world and leaving behind a legacy" (p. 70).

We can see the interconnectedness of narcissism and low EQ as Maccoby (2000) describes unproductive narcissism, "…narcissism can turn unproductive when lacking self-knowledge and restraining anchors, narcissists become unrealistic dreamers…this tendency toward grandiosity and distrust is the Achilles heel of narcissism. Because of it, even brilliant narcissists can come under suspicion for self-involvement, unpredictability, and – in extreme cases – paranoia" (p. 70).

In summary, *Perilous* leaders possessed enormous potential for they were in many ways as talented as *Remarkable* leaders (see Chap. 2). However, they were inherently quite dangerous, too. They could wreak confusion, frustration, and even despair for those who reported to them. But they were perhaps even more dangerous to themselves. They never quite harnessed and channeled their capabilities fully. They endangered their futures by diminishing their accomplishments, resisting constructive feedback, misleading people who try to work collaboratively with them, continuing to seethe in competitive envy, failing to develop talented others, and getting stuck in their dark, self-imposed destinies of "unrequited work."

John was the oldest of three sons whose father was a respected leader of a trade association in the travel industry. With all the comforts of an upper middle class rearing, he was raised to be an emotionally controlled and polite gentleman. The voices of the men in the family remained in a genteel monotone – a stark contrast to his mother's pitched and incessant complaining as she measured her own unrequited life against the accomplishments of other women in her family or neighborhood. She took a daily dose of valium, and John's father drank from crystal tumblers of scotch each evening as he drifted into his own polite removal.

Despite John's ivy league education and early aspiration to become a physician, he abandoned attending medical school for a marriage that ended after a few years. In the mid-1960s while he was casting about for a career that would be both interesting and lucrative, he happened into selling huge main frame computers. While he was quite successful, his ego still craved – and his mother still prodded for the status of – a "professional" career, but his efforts to enter law school were unsuccessful. He remarried and continued in a computer sales and marketing career that never fully gratified him, but he earned enough money to enjoy a comfortable life style.

While John foresaw the advent of the PC market, he failed to follow through on what could have been an immensely satisfying and lucrative entrepreneurial venture. Instead, he spent discretionary cash on fast cars and travel, and he depleted his psychic energy with a pattern of philandering and heavy drinking. Resentful of his second wife's professional pursuits and her resistance to starting a family, this marriage also ended in divorce. While he found happiness in a third marriage and fatherhood, he remained unrequited at work and bitter in the aftermath of his being let go as part of his company's major reorganization.

The *Perilous* Leader

	Ratings		
	Strong	Variable	Weak
I – Leadership competencies			
A. Strategy	✓		
B. Drives results	✓		
C. People		✓	
D. Executive credibility		✓	
II – Emotional intelligence (SO SMART)			
A. Self observation		✓	
B. Self management			✓
C. Attunement		✓	
D. Relationship traction		✓	

End Notes

1   The reader may be familiar with the word "unrequited" in the context of love relationships – love that is not reciprocated or returned by another, i.e., "unrequited love." In this context of leadership types, the word unrequited is used to describe a lack of contentment with one's work-related achievements. This sense of "unrequited work" can feed persistent feelings of career frustration or disappointment – even in the face of considerable accomplishments. In extreme cases, the feeling of unrequited work can result in a major depression.

2   Some *Perilous* leaders stayed in privately held companies where their less positive behavior was tolerated or even excused in the face of their delivering good results. Others experienced a pattern of clashes in the workplace – especially with bosses – that resulted in a checkered work history.

3   In this context, the author uses the term "inner demons" to refer to the relentless and/or haunting psychological issues that perpetuate negative self-talk, i.e., messages to the self that reinforce feelings of insecurity and inadequacy – messages that can prevent people from applying their intellectual and behavioral gifts in bolder and more innovative ways. These messages can also sabotage their chances for forming intimate and lasting love relationships and friendships.

The *Toxic* Business Leader

4

Dictators ride to and fro upon tigers which they dare not dismount. And the tigers are getting hungry.

Winston Churchill

B laine was the second generation CEO of a family-owned professional services company. In this competitive, sales-driven organization, the business producers held top status but, based on their monthly results, they easily fell in and out of favor with Blaine who would publicly chastise those who disappointed him. Despite the company's success, there was a major dark side in this culture fueled by Blaine's constant self-aggrandizement and inappropriate displays of power and dominance.

As a leader, it was difficult for him to retain top talent given the intensity of his micromanagement, profane attacks on people, grandiosity, and obstinacy. Without the benefit of a leadership team or a strategic plan, day-to-day management of the company was chaotic at best. Further, while Blaine projected the image of an impeccable gentleman to the local business community, inside the company, he behaved like a sexual predator with a number of women on the administrative staff.

Beneath the well-groomed surface of this leader, whom many employees described as a "monster," was the wounded heart of an abused and emotionally impoverished child. He was born to privilege but given the preoccupations of his parents, he was denied the emotional caring necessary for him to thrive and become a psychologically healthy and secure adult.

Ultimately, while he worked hard to keep up appearances of success, he would lose several of his most key staff members and clients. The firm would flounder as he strove to perpetuate a perception of growth, rather than dealing with the real issues that jeopardized the company's future.

K.M. Wasylyshyn, *Behind the Executive Door: Unexpected Lessons for Managing Your Boss and Career*, DOI 10.1007/978-1-4614-0376-0_4, © Karol M. Wasylyshyn 2012

Given the serious behavioral issues represented by these business executives and their intensely de-moralizing effects on others, this leadership type was name *Toxic*. It was not uncommon for employees to use words like *strange, weird*, and *bizarre* to describe them. We can think of *Toxic* leaders like Blaine as a negative extension of *Perilous* leaders. Those in this sample were smart and even gifted in the narrow range of their business niche. However, serious psychological issues overwhelmed their ability to channel intellectual resources and business knowledge in a consistent and productive manner.[1] A review of (1) life history, (2) psychological testing, (3) leadership competency, and (4) coaching notes data will provide a fuller understanding of this *Toxic* leadership type.

Life History

The *Toxic* leaders in this sample shared a few life history facts (1) self-absorbed, accomplished parents who could use corporal discipline, (2) strong expectations of them to achieve at a high level, (3) at least a college education – many received advanced degrees, (4) emotionally rocky marriages, (5) no more than two children with whom they had strained relationships, and (6) checkered career histories – unless they were business owners.

Similar to *Perilous* leaders, *Toxic* leaders experienced their share of difficulties in accomplishing the psychosocial tasks of each of the eight Eriksonian stages. Stage 1 (birth–1 year) physical needs were met but many of these leaders grew up in an emotionally bland home atmosphere with little overt emotional expression from their parents. In some cases, this lack of positive emotional sustenance was mild. In others, as with Blaine at the beginning of this chapter and Cate (see sidebar), the emotional deprivation was significant. The resulting problems with trust severely limited the ability of these leaders to form trusting, lasting relationships with others either at work or in their personal lives.

For these *Toxic* leaders the Stage 2 (ages 1–3) task of taking independent action and Stage 3 (ages 3–5) task of initiating more goal-oriented behavior were complicated by parents who were either overly critical or distracted by their own pursuits. As leaders then, they could be plagued by feelings of doubt and shame that they would defend against with retreating or attacking behaviors.

It's difficult to speculate further about the lasting effects of these preschool experiences. This is because these leaders were, for the most part, evasive and/or had defensively blocked specific memories of their earliest years.

For example, it was not uncommon for *Toxic* leaders in their history-taking meetings with me to make comments like, "I really don't remember anything about my childhood" or "Those early events don't really have any relevance for who I am now." A few who were significantly less defensive made comments such as, "I know there are connections between what happened in my childhood and now but it's too painful for me to talk about it."[2]

In Stage 4 (ages 6–11), many *Toxic* leaders realized they were smart enough to get through school without too much effort and that was a good thing because most of them wanted to move onto bigger things. Some even discovered that they had special intellectual gifts. The problem was that many used their brain power as more of a weapon than a tool, i.e., it often manifested as aggressive questioning or debate. Hence, the early seeds of their intellectual obstinacy and/or arrogance were sown. Many proved to be discipline problems in school acting out in class with too much talking or tussling with others whom they resented for various reasons.

As with *Perilous* leaders, developmental milestones did not unfold smoothly in Stage 5 (ages 12–18) for *Toxic* leaders. The combination of parental expectations and their own hyper-competitive or muted achievement orientation left an emotional residue that did not bode well for effective leadership later. Regarding their emerging identities, some of these leaders had consistently expansive images of their futures, some see-sawed between confidence and doubt, and others as one leader said, "…just wanted to get through to something." Nearly half of these leaders had early experiences with alcohol and recreational drugs and described the calming effects of them. Their early dating experiences tended to be more about gratification than the discovery of another person.

By Stage 6 (ages 18–35), these *Toxic* leaders can perhaps be best described as ambivalently intimate with both their work and their personal relationships. Regarding work, the majority of them – especially those who had pursued advanced degrees – had identified a particular industry and career path. Some of these leaders and others of them, too had had jobs with multiple employers but eventually settled into one company.[3] Others had founded or joined successful privately held or family-owned businesses. With no oversight or board scrutiny, some of these leaders proved to be among the most *Toxic*.[4]

There were a number of behaviors among these *Toxic* leaders that strained their personal, as well as their work-related relationships. These included unpredictable mood swings, harsh criticism, angry outbursts bordering on tantrums, extreme self-centeredness, arrogance, and the inability to express tender emotion or caring. For the most part, their personal relationships were tepid and lacking in true intimacy. Some of the most powerful of these leaders, cheated on their marital partners but this behavior was more about the ability to seduce and to be gratified than the search for an emotionally compatible partner. More will be said about relationships under the Psychological Testing section below.

Not a single one of the *Toxic* leaders in this sample exhibited character-istic Stage 7 (ages 35–55) behavior focused on generativity, i.e., efforts to guide the next generation.[5] I would like to remain hopeful that by the time they reach the outer age limit of this stage, they will have had experiences and/or realizations that promote a level of emotional maturity that will foster this type of behavior. To date, the behaviors that got in the way of these leaders' generative behavior included: self-absorption, dominance, ego-centrism, intellectual arrogance, need for affirmation, narrow-mind-edness, problems with impulse control, limited ability to tolerate frustra-tion, grandiosity, hostility, and aloofness.

Like *Perilous* leaders, the majority of *Toxic* leaders in the sample, were having difficulty in making Stage 8 (ages 55–death) progress. Specifically, they were not integrating their career experiences in ways that could be gratifying or that reinforced the likelihood of their honoring their accom-plishments. Remnants of anger, grudges, and an ongoing disconnected-ness with others clogged their abilities to put their careers in full perspective. Significantly for some, the impending loss of power as they approached retirement also had emotionally debilitating effects. Unless these leaders find ways to resolve their anger, tone down the belittling effects of their dominance and arrogance, discover meaningful avocational pursuits, and resolve the hurts they have spread over their personal relationships, theirs is not a satisfying picture of the future.[6]

Psychological Testing Results

There were notable differences in the psychological assessment results among *Toxic* leaders and both *Remarkable* and *Perilous* leaders. To sim-plify here, I'll focus comparative comments between the *Remarkable* and *Toxic* leaders in this sample.

On the Watson–Glaser Critical Thinking Appraisal, the scores of *Toxic* leaders were not as consistently high as those of the *Remarkable* leaders. Based on testing feedback conversations held with these leaders, two fac-tors provided at least some information about their depressed scores. First, many of these leaders failed to concentrate as fully and carefully as they needed to on the test (*I really couldn't relate to this test* or, *I filled it out on a plane when I was pretty jet-lagged*). Second, some of them were just not as talented in this area as the *Remarkable* leaders. For other of these leaders, their lower scores were a function of both of these factors. Of note, is that whatever the explanation was for their lower scores (at average or below average ranges when compared to Executive and Managerial norms), they were not especially concerned about it. In the words of one *Toxic* leader, "This doesn't really relate to what I need to do my job well."

Regarding the behavioral preferences of these *Toxic* leaders, as measured by the Myers-Briggs Type Indicator, they were evenly split between extraversion and introversion. Several of them tested as a combination of extraverted and introverted behavior preferences. These leaders were often perceived as more enigmatic and/or hard to understand for people could never be sure where the *Toxic* leader was coming from or what was expected of them. They were also split between a preference for focusing on present priorities and results versus a more intuitive and future orientation. An overwhelming majority of these leaders preferred facts and data for decision-making and had little patience for or focus on the feelings and concerns of others. Finally, they were also evenly split on comfort with ambiguity versus preferring a more orderly and systematic approach to work-related objectives.

Unlike *Remarkable* leaders, the majority of these leaders' thinking about managing people, as measured by the Life Styles Inventory (LSI), showed elevation in the Aggressive/Defensive thinking style. This style is focused most on getting tasks completed and the dimensions within it involve: (1) oppositional behavior, (2) an appetite for power, (3) being competitive – even at the expense of others, and (4) a perfectionistic approach. Many of these leaders had high scores on at least two of these dimensions – usually power and competition.

Of these *Toxic* leaders, some displayed an elevation in the Passive/Defensive thinking style. However, there were no common themes among the specific behavioral dimensions of avoidance, dependence, conventional thinking, and approval-seeking.

When *Toxic* leaders showed any elevations in the behavior dimensions of the Constructive thinking style, it was Achievement. However, the achievement orientation of these leaders was often more about their personal achievements than those attained by their teams or assistance they might have given peers.

Toxic leaders also presented variable results on the NEO-PI-R, a measure based on the Big 5 Factor Theory of personality and one of the measures used in the empirical research discussed in Chap. 1. Compared to *Remarkable* leaders, these leaders were (1) more neurotic – inclined to experience negative feelings, act impulsively and/or display anxiety, anger, hostility, and prone toward depression; (2) able to establish rapport with others but usually with less warmth and optimism; (3) less likely to express their feelings or ideas; (4) less trusting, altruistic, compliant, and tender-minded; and (5) less disciplined in terms of planning, organizing, completing tasks efficiently.

Regarding emotional intelligence (EQ), *Toxic* leaders had lower EQ scores than *Remarkable* leaders as measured by the Emotional Quotient Inventory (EQ-i), another assessment tool used in the empirical research described in Chap. 1. For the most part, the EQ scores of these leaders were below the average range.

Unlike *Remarkable* leaders, they were considerably less self observant so they lacked an honest appraisal of their strengths and weaknesses. Their perceptions of how they impacted others were often seriously off the mark. They had little capacity to modulate their impulses or censor negative emotions like anger, frustration, and disappointment. They were known for outbursts that abruptly ended meetings or set off hostile interactions that interrupted progress on key objectives.

Attunement to the needs or concerns of others was also seriously lacking among these *Toxic* leaders. For the most part, they were so fixated on their own priorities that even family members complained of a pattern of neglect and of their receiving harsh insults and relentless criticism. When they behaved empathetically, it was more manipulative than real. For example, one business Vice President aware of a subordinate's stress over a critically ill father, urged the direct report to take time to visit his ailing father. The boss knew that he was about to hire a new team member who could readily cover for – and maybe even replace – the team member sent traveling to see his parent.

The work relationships of these *Toxic* leaders were primarily transactional based on what they expected and needed people to do for them versus their making any personal connections. An extreme example of this was the Founder/CEO of a professional services firm who required a 24/7 instantaneous response to his emails from all this direct reports. For the most part such leaders had minimal interest in other people's achievements, families, travels, or concerns – unless their appearing to do so served them some immediate purpose like establishing rapport with a prospective new customer. They were often incapable of expressing tender emotion or relating to others in a loving, caring manner. However, they were able to "fake" such behavior especially in the seduction phase of a customer relationship but they were ill-equipped to sustain close relationships – especially with people inside their organizations.

In their personal relationships, *Toxic* leaders could be promiscuous, as was Blaine, and preyed on others in search of their own pleasure and personal conquests. While most stayed married, these relationships were impoverished emotionally. One spouse said of her husband, "The only way our marriage survives is based on the fact that he travels most of the time. I can stand him in small doses." Further, these leaders often had contentious relationships with their children most of whom had grown weary of parental domination and criticism. Most of these leaders had few, if any, truly close friends.

Core Leadership Competencies

In terms of the four essential leadership competencies (strategy, driving results, managing people, and executive credibility), *Toxic* leaders had significant difficulties in each of these competency areas. However, the specific nature of these difficulties varied given all the potential permutations of their erratic thoughts and behavioral problems.

Strategy

Toxic leaders often had difficulty with or were literally turned off by the demands of formulating a sound strategic plan. Some lacked the synthetic thinking skill for it. Others were not able to muster the discipline, rigor, and patience required for effective strategic planning. Like Blaine, many of these leaders prided themselves on not having or needing to have a business strategy because they were so knowledgeable about their businesses. Invariably, they rationalized or defended against criticism by maintaining that they ran their companies or business units on "gut instinct" that continued to serve them well.

Further, some of these *Toxic* leaders were so intellectually arrogant that they made strategic decisions in isolation and then resented the time it took to achieve alignment with their leadership teams. This also made it more difficult for them to make nimble strategic adjustments. Others' ideas were arbitrarily shot down or otherwise diminished because *Toxic* leaders were close-minded, unable to take the perspective of another, and were compelled to impose their own ideas.

Some *Toxic* leaders were so preoccupied with orderliness, achieving perfection, and controlling every facet of their work lives, they were too uptight and rigid for collegial discussions of strategy. As leaders, they could get things done but they were more focused on their tactical "to do" lists than on making sound and timely strategic decisions.

Driving Results

There were *Toxic* leaders like Blaine who projected an attitude of invulnerability based on their commanding knowledge of their businesses and a history of considerable success. Whether they could sustain the same level of results in twenty-first century business conditions became increasingly questionable. The complexity of economic, demographic, political, diversity, and generational issues – to cite just a few – required coordinated thought and action.

This was nigh impossible for many *Toxic* leaders. Their future results were compromised by their considerable mental and behavioral limitations. In public companies, these leaders, like Cate (see sidebar) will begin to be replaced. In private and family-owned businesses, things may need to reach a near disastrous crescendo before leadership changes will be made.

Managing People

Given their psychological issues, *Toxic* leaders rarely motivated, inspired, or managed people effectively. On the contrary, they demotivated, depressed, and mismanaged many who often felt trapped especially if they were in a depressed job market. The primary managerial lever of some *Toxic* leaders was monetary – which helped them retain talented people for a time anyway. However, rather than garnering the commitment and respect of these employees, *Toxic* bosses were often the focal point of derisive gossip. Further, employee productivity was eroded by the time they spent venting about their bosses' limitations as leaders.

As indicated above, these business executives were fundamentally unable to lead high performing teams. Given their problems with trust, they were prone toward maladaptive behavior such as playing team members against each other. These *Toxic* leaders could also turn on others quickly and inexplicably move people in and out of the "penalty box." In these circumstances, team members braced themselves for the leader's sudden, swift displeasure that resulted in their being cast into the metaphorical Siberia where they would languish – until the leader needed them again (see *Stranded* in Chap. 9).

Further, with little understanding of or patience for team-based leadership, some of these leaders actually lead global enterprises without a leadership team at all. Leading from a command-and-control perspective, they preferred face-to-face interactions with their key lieutenants whom they expected to implement their directives. They were caustic and otherwise punishing when this did not happen. Theirs was primarily an intermittent type of reinforcement leaving direct reports never certain of whether they would be stroked or slapped.[7]

As with *Perilous* leaders but often to a greater degree, there were serious people management issues related to the lack of clarity regarding roles, expectations, accountabilities, and deadlines. Since they were not especially effective at giving timely and candid feedback, employees often lacked a clear sense of how they were doing and received little, if any, guidance about what they needed to improve. As one humorous manager once said, "We practice the mushroom management theory here – just keep us in the dark and throw manure on us hoping that we'll grow."

Finally, *Toxic* leaders were limited in their effectiveness on a whole range of talent management issues including hiring the best people, assimilating them well, promotion decisions, people development, and performance feedback. Also, given their underlying grandiosity or inadequacy – or perhaps a combination of both – these leaders often failed to develop someone to succeed them. Depending on the level of their role in the business, this posed considerable difficulty in ensuring a smooth leadership transition and in maintaining positive financial results.

Executive Credibility

The credibility of *Toxic* leaders was significantly flawed.[8] For the most part, they had serious problems with communication, consistency, and courage. The combination of their flawed thinking, erratic behavior, and deep psychological issues usually destroyed the credibility of *Toxic* leaders within their organizations. However, like Blaine and Cate, they were able to sustain some aura of respectability externally where exposure to them through professional organizations or non-profit boards, e.g., was minimal.

Regarding communication, there were problems regarding both content and delivery. With their thoughts often scrambled, still forming, and/or ever-changing, these leaders were not known for compelling large or small group presentations, and the extent of their self-references was a major turn-off. While somewhat more effective face-to-face, direct reports found they needed to keep verifying what they heard to ensure their alignment with a *Toxic* boss.

Consistency proved to be particularly challenging for these *Toxic* bosses. The combination of behavior preferences, personality factors, and challenging business dynamics (that made these bosses even more erratic), created what one astute General Manager in a global company described as a "whip lash" culture. People in this culture often began meetings with questions like, "*Where is he on this issue today?*" The stress of such inconsistency contributed to a number of high potential employees requesting transfers into different business units – or, being more responsive to calls from executive recruiters.

Typically, these *Toxic* executives were not known for courageous stands on people or business issues. Regarding the latter, they were considered to be too muddled in their thinking and behavior to be fully credible. Regarding the former, high potential people in particular learned that they needed to take care of their own branding. They made a point of forming relationships with their HR managers, as well as with other business leaders in their companies. Others, especially if they were employed in large public companies, just decided to wait-it-out believing their pointed comments to the right people would eventually result in their *Toxic* leader being replaced and/or removed from the company. In this era of increased behavioral scrutiny, this has become an effective strategy – assuming care is taken in orchestrating what gets said to whom when.

Coaching Notes

For most *Toxic* leaders, the suggestion that they could benefit from executive coaching was definitely experienced as an indictment of their capabilities. This ran very much counter to their ego-centric and expansive self images. However, since most of these individuals were in companies where coaching was part of an ongoing leadership development initiative, it would have been a political faux pas for them to outright reject participation.

An analysis of these coaching engagements in my sample of 300 cases, revealed that 69% of the 60 *Toxic* participants "faked" their involvement. In other words, they entered coaching with a belief that they had no need for it and therefore, there would be no value in it. Another 15% benefitted indirectly through the coaching of their boss.[9] Another 15% did outright refuse to participate but I had ample observation of and collateral information to categorize them as *Toxic*. Pitiful as it might sound, the remaining 1% involved one *Toxic* leader who knew he needed and actually benefitted from coaching. Based on these data, I decided that coaching was best reserved for high potential individuals who were invested in their ongoing growth and development. I have referred to this as the Olympian model of executive coaching (Wasylyshyn 2003).

Given this era of scrutinizing the behavior *how* dimension of leadership, it is getting harder for *Toxic* leaders to reach and/or retain senior executive roles in global for profit companies. Based on their intelligence and technical credentials, they may get hired by prestigious companies but they eventually get weeded out due to their behavior issues. Some, who possess critical technical competence, may maintain employment in these settings – but they will most likely be isolated in individual contributor roles versus holding senior leadership responsibilities.

As indicated earlier, *Toxic* leaders can be found in privately held or family-owned business environments. This is not to say that there aren't also very capable – including *Remarkable* – leaders in these business settings. The point here is that there can be degrees of tolerance for ineffective leadership behavior and/or strong attitudes of familial entitlement that dominate considerations of who gets to lead in these settings. With no higher source to "report to" such as a Board of Directors, *Toxic* leaders can remain in leadership roles for extended periods.

As leaders, they can be among the unproductive narcissists preoccupied with aspirations for their success, visibility, fame, and instant gratification that the needs or concerns of others are rarely, if ever, a priority. Given these dominant behaviors, they fail abysmally at leading – or even at forming effective teams (Maccoby 2000).

Unproductive narcissistic leaders can feign caring and connection with others but most often this is exploitative manipulation with the single-minded goal of achieving their purposes. They not only lack genuine empathy for others, they can envy others or mistakenly believe that others envy them. While they can "play" and manipulate executives who are senior to them, they are often described by peers and others as haughty, cold, and/or arrogant.

In summary, the leadership competency problems, low EQ, and behavioral issues of *Toxic* leaders seriously limited their ability to lead effectively. Even when they were intellectually gifted and especially knowledgeable about their businesses, their problematic behavior left their companies in constant jeopardy, demoralized employees, and encased company cultures in an atmosphere of relentless tension and frustration.

Cate was the oldest of three children born to high achieving parents both of whom had completed ivy league educations. While her mother had aspired to a professional career, she capitulated to her mother's pressure to remain home and raise her offspring. This was a source of lifelong resentment for Cate's mother who, like her father, provided Cate with little physical or emotional affection. A "good girl," Cate performed well in school and did not risk the wrath of her impatient and relentlessly demanding parents. She never complained even as her parents traveled extensively leaving Cate and her two siblings with an ever-changing cast of caregivers.

Rarely praised for her academic success or potential, Cate questioned her innate ability but she was nevertheless intent on doing something "unique" with her life. However, an early marriage and her need for financial stability and independence influenced her acceptance of the first good job offer she received. This was a managerial trainee role in a global manufacturing company where she remained for 21 years. She gravitated toward Finance where she distinguished herself in the handling of a number of complex projects. However, as she was promoted into roles that required the formation and management of global teams, her career began to flounder. While an excellent strategist and problem-solver, her people management limitations became increasingly apparent. Her direct reports experienced her as overly demanding, reactive, punishing, and without empathy for the fatigue and stress in the team.

While Cate represented the company well in various community-based organizations, her relationships inside the company – especially with those who reported to her –deteriorated badly. She had received candid feedback from a coach but her direct reports saw no signs that she had internalized it and worse, they needed to unify in a resistance to her efforts to determine who had said what in this data-gathering process. As she became more anxious and defensive about her performance, members of her team filed grievances about her unfair and harassing treatment of them. Cate had become trapped in a career that simply was not the best fit given her many real strengths – and limitations too. Ultimately, she was separated from the company.

The *Toxic* Leader

| | Ratings | | |
	Strong	Variable	Weak
I – Leadership competencies			
A. Strategy		✓	
B. Drives results		✓	
C. People			✓
D. Executive credibility			✓
II – Emotional intelligence (SO SMART)			
A. Self observation			✓
B. Self management			✓
C. Attunement			✓
D. Relationship traction			✓

End Notes

[1] In my clinical opinion many of these executives suffered from undiagnosed bipolar illness, psychopathy or personality disorders that included narcissistic character disorder and borderline personality disorder. Further information on these mental disorders is available in the Diagnostic and Statistical Manual of Mental Disorders (DSM-IV-TR).

[2] There were some *Toxic* leaders who had sought out psychotherapy and through that experience received important insights about the psychogenic basis of their less effective leadership and personal relationship behaviors.

[3] Beginning in the early twenty-first century, we began to see a shift in executive career paths such that a more nomadic profile was not unusual – and may even have become desirable in an ever growing technological age that valued diversity of experiences. This shift will likely continue.

[4] Through my consulting experiences, I have seen many *Toxic* leaders in both public and privately-held or family owned businesses. Regarding the privately-held or family-run sector, there are many organizations that are being lead by splendidly competent *Remarkable* leaders, as well as flawed *Toxic* leaders.

[5] This is not to say that anyone considered to be a *Toxic* leader is incapable of or necessarily disinclined to guide and/or groom members of the next generation. Those who discover the value of this activity, as well as their own way of conveying the wisdom and experiences they have accrued in their careers, can achieve Stage 7 generativity.

[6] Many of these leaders could benefit from psychotherapy, a coach, or a trusted spiritual advisor who can hold up a mirror and help them see what they need to see behaviorally as they make this major life transition. In the presence of such information and their intention to make necessary behavior changes, they can ease themselves toward greater contentment – but it will take a strongly committed effort to do so.

[7] There are three primary types of motivation (1) positive reinforcement whereby leaders are encouraging and focused on affirming positive results, (2) negative reinforcement whereby leaders are primarily judgmental, critical and disinclined to offer affirmation, and (3) intermittent reinforcement whereby subordinates are never quite sure what feedback they will receive from the boss. This is the least effective form of motivation, even worse than negative reinforcement.

8   Many of these leaders, especially those who delivered strong business results, had long tenures of employment – despite their leadership flaws. In this era of scrutinizing executive behavior, blatantly flawed executives are increasingly more at risk.

9   My coaching model involves a close collaboration with a coachee's boss. Of the 300 cases in my research sample, 20% were categorized as *Remarkable*, 60% as *Perilous*, and 20% as *Toxic*.

Leadership Type Exercise: What Type of Leader Is Your Boss?

5

What type of leader is your boss? Your clarity about this is key in the effort you make to manage him or her more effectively.

The following *Leadership Type Exercise* is a rapid way for you to answer this question.

PLEASE READ THE FOLLOWING THREE CAVEATS BEFORE YOU BEGIN THE *LEADERSHIP TYPE EXERCISE*:

Caveat #1: The result of this exercise provides a *descriptive pattern* of your boss's leadership behavior. It is not a definitive profile of your boss's capabilities as a leader. However, it can be a helpful guide in your consideration of how you might manage your boss more effectively.

Caveat #2: There are limitations to self-administered exercises such as this. If you want to identify a useful and accurate descriptive pattern of your boss's leadership behavior, *mark the statements as objectively as possible*. As a reality check, discuss the result of this exercise with someone else who knows your boss well.

Caveat #3: Once you are satisfied that you have an objective *descriptive pattern* of your boss, you are ready to consider the lessons for managing *Remarkable, Perilous*, and *Toxic* bosses provided in Chaps. 6–8, respectively.

Exercise

Leadership Type Exercise

Instruction for taking this exercise:

- Mark the statements that apply to your boss.
- The statements are grouped in three sections, read ALL of the statements in EACH section and mark the applicable statements in each section.

K.M. Wasylyshyn, *Behind the Executive Door: Unexpected Lessons for Managing Your Boss and Career*, DOI 10.1007/978-1-4614-0376-0_5, © Karol M. Wasylyshyn 2012

- These statements are based on the criteria used to describe the three leadership types – *Remarkable*, *Perilous*, and *Toxic* – described in earlier Chapters of this book.

First Set of Statements

My boss:

___ Has a leadership style that is based primarily on the objective analysis of facts and data; the people issues are a necessary part too – but a distant second.

___ Forms strong strategies and a compelling picture of the future but getting people excited and aligned about what he/she sees is the hard part.

___ Can keep adjusting his/her thoughts even after a path forward on an issue has been decided; there could be better consistency between what he/she says and does.

___ Thinks he/she is quite self-aware and tuned into him/herself emotionally but he/she gets feedback to the contrary.

___ Believes he/she does a good job of using both positive and negative emotions but after team meetings, for example, people can feel deflated by his/her criticism or missed opportunities for him/her to pump up the team.

___ Will not let organizational politics or other culture factors get in the way of achieving business results.

___ Knows emotional intelligence is a focus in leadership thinking now but he/she is not focused on being empathic about others' concerns.

___ Has work relationships that are primarily transactional, i.e., they're more about getting things done than forming personal ties.

___ Believes empowerment needs to be earned; once people have earned it, then he/she is more willing to delegate fully to them.

___ Sets a course of action, and doesn't like being second-guessed on it.

___ Doesn't like ambiguity – unless it's the ambiguity he/she has created.

___ Can show some degree of anxiety or uncertainty when he/she gets new and/or expanded responsibility because he/she needs to feel a sense of mastery and control to lead effectively.

___ Is more focused on work/career than on personal relationships.

___ Expects people to work out the conflicts that can crop up so his/her intervention is not needed.

___ Favors working independently but is OK working with the team.

Second Set of Statements

My boss:

___ Forms a strategy for the business or functional area he/she is leading and prefers to do this with his/her leadership team.

___ Drives high quality results in a cost-effective and timely manner.

___ Gets the right people in the right roles and sets the conditions for them to be successful.

___ Gives a lot of positive feedback and motivational support to direct reports.

___ Will always do the right thing even if that means jeopardizing his/her career.

___ Spends time planning how to best communicate with employees at all levels in the organization about our strategy and the objectives that must be met to achieve the strategy.

___ Expects bold action of him/herself and values this in others. Prefers people ask for forgiveness – not permission.

___ Is more focused on leveraging his/her strengths than worrying too much about his/her weaknesses.

___ Will spend at least as much time trying to win people's hearts as trying to win their minds.

___ Makes a real effort to find out what others are concerned about and their aspirations as well.

___ Expects people to be accountable so it's easy for him/her to delegate fully.

___ Builds and motivates high performing teams; this is one of his/her top skills as a leader.

___ Forms deep and lasting relationships with people inside and outside the company.

Third Set of Statements

My boss:

___ Sometimes acts like business success would be a lot easier if it weren't for the people who need to be lead.

___ Is more intuitive than strategic.

___ Can create chaos and there can be a lack of consistency between what he/she says and does.

___ Doesn't focus on other people's feelings about their work or things going on in their lives; probably wouldn't know what to do with that kind of information.

___ Thinks people waste time on company politics and organization culture issues.

___ When it comes to something like empathy, he/she expects people to get into his/her shoes once in awhile.

___ Could be better at delegation but this is hard because he/she believes no one's going to do things as well as he/she would do them.

___ Believes high performing teams get the job done – they don't need retreats or other team-building experiences to make them effective.

___ Values work as the most important thing in life. Getting close to other people is just not his/her thing.

___ Can be stubborn once he/she has set a course of action. People can bring him/her data supporting a different view, but if his/her gut says "no," it's going to be no.

___ Doesn't sleep well when he/she gets a new job. His/her fears about failure can return with a vengeance.

___ Is basically a conflict avoider. He/she doesn't have the time, patience, or skill to deal with negative issues effectively. This has adverse effects on productive team work.

After completing the exercise:

1. After you have marked all the statements that apply to your boss, turn to Appendix A to see which set of statements refer to which leadership type.

2. Then return to your marked pages and ask yourself the following three questions:
   - In what section did I have the *most* checks?
     Interpretation: This indicates your boss's leadership type.
   - In what section did I have the *fewest* checks?
     Interpretation: This indicates your boss's least preferred way of leading.
   - In which sections did I have a *similar number* of checks?
     Interpretation: Your boss is not distinctly one type. His/her leadership behavior typically varies depending on the confluence of business and/or personal factors.

3. You are now ready to consider the lessons for managing your boss. Read the appropriate chapter (or chapters if your boss does not have a distinct type):
   - For *Remarkable* boss – Chap. 6

- For *Perilous* boss – Chap. 7
- For *Toxic* boss – Chap. 8

Some of these lessons may resonate for you and some may not. Spend more time considering the ones that do, and then plan how you will put them into action in dealing with your boss.

Prelude to Using Lessons for Managing Your Boss

The following lessons are presented as a catalyst and in the spirit of guidance, i.e., guiding your discovery of actions that will enable you to forge a more productive – and potentially satisfying – relationship with your boss. The behavioral guidance provided in these lessons is unlikely to map perfectly to your boss relationship, but there should be enough in these lessons to spark a different approach on your part.

In the macro, your managing a boss more effectively should enable you to:

1. Deepen a positive and learning relationship with a *Remarkable* boss
2. Reinforce the best behavior and minimize the less effective and discontented behaviors of a *Perilous* boss
3. Minimize a *Toxic* leader's most destructive effects on you and perhaps on others as well

Finally, if you think this sounds like an attempt to develop your coaching skill – you're right. In this twenty-first-century business climate, the most effective and harmonious working relationships will necessarily involve mutual learning and coaching between leaders and the gifted people reporting to them.

There are many reasons for this including (1) the increasing numbers of younger people who are managing others older than they, (2) geographically dispersed teams, and (3) the cultural differences among people in business organizations – differences that must be learned, respected, and integrated into organizations that are intent on evolving new and more flexible models for workplace productivity and sustained success.

I offer these lessons for managing bosses as a potential primer for people who want to make their time at work – all those considerable hours at work – more productive and satisfying than you may have ever imagined possible. As Whyte (1994) said, "The split between what is nourishing at work and what is agonizing is the very chasm from which our personal destiny emerges (p. 5)."

APPLYING THE UNDERSTANDING OF BUSINESS LEADER BEHAVIOR

PRELUDE   Unexpected Lessons for Managing Your Boss

The description of three prevalent leadership types – *Remarkable*, *Perilous*, and *Toxic* – plus the identification of a boss's leadership type (or mix of types) using the Leadership Type Exercise in Chapter 5, provide the foundation for considering ways to manage your boss more effectively.

Surely any consideration of ways to manage a boss is vast, elusive, and plagued by the complexities of interpersonal relationships. What is offered in these lessons is not a relationship elixir. Rather, what is offered -- humbly and with the strong belief in the potential for improving these relationships -- is a start, a provocation, an encouragement, a match with which to strike a flame for building or renewing boss relationships.

The lessons embedded in the following three chapters have been culled from the author's executive coaching and advisory experiences. While many tools and approaches were used with executive clients to accelerate their leadership effectiveness, these tools also bear promise for improving both career prospects and boss relationships.

Some of these lessons will resonate more than others so focus on these first for immediate boss management clues. Some may not hit the mark at all – at least upon a first reading. Push those aside for now but return to them for each has been well tried, tested and proven useful. Readiness is the key. As a CFO once commented, "You and I had been over that point about solitude – I just wasn't ready to hear it. Now that I've cleared the static within, I understand the importance of solitude – the power of my carving out quiet time for reflection on the big issues and the implications of that for my being a more effective leader."

There are a few caveats regarding the viability of managing a boss more effectively. First, if you cannot park your ego at the door, you'll need to resolve or seek help with this before you even attempt to apply any of these lessons. Second, if the chemistry between your boss and you is irrevocably negative, none of these lessons is likely to be as helpful as getting another boss. And third, if any of your current work-related issues are more a function of a misfit between your role and/or the company culture and you, your energy may best be spent on seeking a more suitable career situation.

Further, there is a huge distance between 1) a lesson described and 2) a lesson applied. What makes the difference between someone grasping a lesson and using that lesson in a rewarding way? Is it relevance of the lesson to the learner's situation? Is it the learner's ability to concentrate and apply key learning points? Is it the credibility of the teacher? The need of the learner? While all of these factors are important none are as potent as this: your intention to do this hard thing.

It is your unwavering and unselfish commitment to helping your boss be more effective as a leader. This is not about sucking up. This does not mean that your own aspirations are subordinated or neglected. Rather, whatever your aspirations may be, your most effective behavior will be driven by efforts to propel the overall success of the organization and by extension this includes supporting your boss. Embedded in this commitment is the belief that your career success will emerge through concerted efforts that are apolitical, transparent and fuelled by the stellar quality of your work.

Finally, if you discover just one lesson of value, and apply this lesson with the full force of your intention, we have succeeded in our joint effort toward your managing your boss well. I applaud the purity of your intention – and I believe that your efforts will be rewarded in your boss relationship – and in your career.

Managing a *Remarkable* Boss

6

> "God promoted me. I'm so glad now I have a new boss … My new boss looks beyond all my faults and sees my needs. He gave me a new benefits package: grace and mercy. He gave me a brand new pension plan in the eternal."
>
> *Reverend Wilson W. Goode*
> *Former Mayor of Philadelphia*

Putting any faith-based notions aside, Wilson Goode's new boss is *Remarkable* if we consider him metaphorically through the lens of business leadership. Foremost, he is an all empowering boss who does not dictate, micromanage, or criticize. Despite even the most demanding business conditions, he remains accessible for conversation and emotional support any time, day, or night. Despite the mistakes, missed deadlines, mediocre results, or other failings of his direct reports, his respect and affection for them is stolidly unconditional. Transparent and open to scrutiny, he is less ego and more celebrant not just of the success of his employees but of their contentment, peace, and faith in the future. His relationships with the people who "report" to him are enduring and reciprocal.

Primary Premise for Managing a *Remarkable* Boss: The Power of Reciprocity

Managing or becoming a *Remarkable* boss rests significantly on this: the commitment to forming and maintaining a *reciprocal relationship*. This means that both boss and direct report are consistently and relentlessly striving to give as much to the other as each possibly can. Each party benefits from the other – and neither would likely be as successful without the other. An example of such reciprocity is the relationship between the US President (Barack Obama) and the Secretary of State (Hilary Clinton). In business, the relationship between Microsoft Chairman Bill Gates and his CEO Steve

Ballmer is illustrative of such reciprocity with Gates as the innovation genius and Ballmer leading operations.

This *reciprocal working* results in bosses feeling fully supported, direct reports learning/prospering, and organizations succeeding because objectives are met – and usually exceeded. In both thriving and struggling business climates, this reciprocity is the glue that binds and sustains high performing people together. This reciprocal intention replaces the *What's in it for me* question with *What's in it for us*, and from this flows a steady commitment to surpass expectations, promote continued success of the enterprise, and ensure mutually flourishing careers.

Example of Reciprocal Working

When Norm immigrated from the United Kingdom to the United States, he was a young and relatively inexperienced engineer. He joined a small engineering firm that would grow rapidly and eventually emerge as a major player for data center design, construction, and commissioning. Mentored closely by the brilliant founder of the firm, Norm matched his boss's 24/7 pace, mounted an impressive learning curve, applied his unique talents, and achieved the financial stability he desired. Through a tightly reciprocal relationship with his boss, he played a major role in differentiating the firm for its graphical clarity, as well as for the depth and breadth of its technical engineering capabilities.

While working for a *Remarkable* boss is desirable, it is not necessarily smooth, easy, or reassuring. These bosses typically hold themselves and others to exceedingly high-performance standards. Their brand of urgency is characterized by a voracious appetite for genuinely novel solutions, ideas, and processes that will foster distinctive results. They are impatient with the mundane. They are as quick to display displeasure as they are to publicly affirm work well done. In short, working for them requires significant mental, physical, and emotional stamina.

The remainder of this chapter focuses on practical ways to please and manage a *Remarkable* boss.[1] This content is guided by the leadership competencies, emotional intelligence, and behavioral observations of *Remarkable* leaders provided in Chap. 2.[2]

Note: This information should also be useful to readers who want to become *Remarkable* leaders.

Leadership Competencies

Strategy

Since *Remarkable* leaders are typically strong strategically, they value direct reports who can stretch the boss's thinking by recognizing patterns, anticipating business issues, synthesizing strategic thoughts, and responding to marketplace conditions proactively. Further, individuals who cue bosses regarding strategic flaws, barriers, or potentially insurmountable political hurdles in the company also score points with a *Remarkable* boss. Anyone who aspires to manage and/or engage a boss in this way must prioritize the necessary time to read, think, and immerse themselves strategically, as well as to establish and regularly tap into a strong network of industry and industry-related contacts for strategic input.

Once a strategy has been set, there are myriad opportunities to help the boss ensure its implementation – especially if one was involved in its creation. In their insightful and pragmatic book, McKnight et al. (2010) write, "Most approaches to strategy implementation fail because strategy is created at one level (the top) and handed off to another (the middle and bottom). We believe that to improve strategy implementation, you have to involve employees extensively in *creating* the strategy, and senior managers have to become involved in *executing* – as well as formulating – the strategy" (p. 16).

When a direct report is in true reciprocal rhythm with a boss on strategy, there is a shared searching for the truth – the business truth that both informs direction and ensures strategic execution. Depending on the boss's role, the strategy may relate to the overall company, a business unit, a department, or a functional area such as Human Resources or Finance. This does not matter. What matters for employees who are trying to manage and/or influence their boss's best strategic impact is their active pursuit of ways to do this.[3]

One of the most immediate ways to do this is to inject strategic comments, questions, or thoughts into regularly scheduled 1:1 meetings with a boss. There can be an element of surprise – and even delight – for a boss when this happens. However, because these face to face meetings are usually consumed by pressing tactical issues related to the work at hand, the direct report must make a concerted effort to break this pattern. Understandably, this can be anxiety-provoking or feel unnatural at first, but provided one has done his/her strategy homework, these feelings should abate – especially given a boss's budding recognition of value in the efforts being made. These efforts can influence (1) new thinking that enriches a forming strategy, (2) refined thinking related to an existing strategy, (3) more serious consideration of internal political hurdles, and (4) just-in-time identification of external threats.

Example of Branding One's
Strategic Potential

Robert was a well-respected CFO of a midsize financial services company. Imminently capable and widely respected by both his boss, the CEO, and Board members, he aspired to become CEO. While capable of strategic thinking and planning, his reflexive caution, risk aversion, and low-key manner combined to mask these capabilities. For him to remain as a viable CEO succession candidate, he would have to stretch out of his tactical/operational comfort zone and raise the level of his discussions with both his boss and the Board.

Robert took this on as a serious development goal and worked with an executive coach and a communications expert for a year. A major coaching focus was conveying his strategic thinking on future business challenges, as well as the strategic implications of current issues within Finance. With his self-imposed pressure and the help of external resources, he made notable progress and continued as a CEO succession candidate.

Anyone desirous of managing his/her boss in this manner – and simultaneously conveying their own potential as a strategic thinker will, like Robert, have to escape their inner Doing Demon. In other words, there will be an intentional moving away from tactical issues toward strategic involvement. Eventually, the lion share of tactical execution will be delegated to others. This is not dump-and-run delegation; rather, it is another example of boss–subordinate reciprocity. Specifically, the delegators avoid being locked into a tactical – and career-limiting – plateau while their direct reports are developed through the activities delegated to them.

To assess whether or not you are trapped in the tactical, see The Doing Demon Quiz in Appendix B.

Driving Results

DePree (1989), the former Chairman and CEO of Herman Miller Business Furniture wrote, "The first responsibility of a leader is to define reality. The last is to say thank you. In between the two, the leader must become a servant and a debtor" (p. 11). There is coherence between DePree's notion of *defining reality* and *Remarkable* leaders' talent for setting a clear strategic direction. The *saying thank you* part of his leader formulation is inevitable given the emotional intelligence of *Remarkable* leaders. His reference to the leader as "servant" is based on a philosophy of leadership first articulated by Robert K. Greenleaf in a 1970 essay, "The Servant as Leader." In his view, leaders are significantly focused on responding to the needs of those they lead. They are humble and intent on building working communities of co-constructed meaning and results.

Remarkable leaders are modern day conceptualizations of this servant leader model. They are emblematic of what Collins termed a "level 5" leader – one who combines relentlessness and humility (2001). Given the combination of their emotional and social intelligence,[4] *Remarkable* leaders strive to be attuned to all stakeholders, and they form loyal relationships with enough grace points in the bank to survive problems or disappointments.

In the academic realm, we find what is perhaps one of the best examples of servant leadership in what is called civic engagement. In 2010, Widener University in Chester Pennsylvania was ranked by *Newsweek* as one of the top ten colleges and universities in the nation for civic-minded students. Widener has led a collaborative effort of six different colleges and universities to open a college access center for the community, opened a small business development center, and spearheaded a $50 million economic revitalization development in Chester, Pennsylvania, one of the nation's most economically challenged cities.

Example of Servant Leader Driving Results

Upon becoming President of Widener University in Chester, PA, James T. Harris III said, "To paraphrase Dickens: We have the best of times. We have the worst of times. But this is more than the tale of two communities. This is a tale of how a University can use its resources, energies, and influence to bridge the gap between those two communities." Harris's leadership has been guided by a comprehensive strategic plan that included his senior administrators, deans, faculty members, students, and Chester community members in the creation phase. This level of inclusion has abetted the completion of a rolling set of strategic objectives.

Returning to DePree, his use of the word "art" influenced the author's creation of a lesson designed to highlight an ideal sequence of leadership behavior – for driving results. In this sequence, leaders *articulate* first, *react* to progress being made, and then *teach* what went well and what did not as a way of reinforcing others' ongoing development. To assess the extent to which your boss is leading ART-fully, see the lesson, *Using A.R.T. to Achieve Peak Performance from Others*, in Appendix C.

Exercise

Assessing the ART-FUL Managing of Others

Ask yourself these questions: *Is my boss managing others ART-fully* (articulate–react–teach sequence) *or is he/she managing like a RAT* (react–articulate–teach sequence)? The goal is to ensure that a boss stays in the ART-FUL sequence.

Because lack of clarity is often a major issue, ART can be a useful tool in maintaining clarity and traction on goals. Even *Remarkable* bosses can benefit from direct reports who manage them by making sure they:

- A – articulate – convey clear objectives (the WHAT), accountabilities (the WHO), and deadlines (the WHEN)
- R – react – review progress on goals in time for necessary adjustments to be made
- T – teach – conduct the debriefs of initiatives that went well or bad – as a way of reinforcing key learning points for the future

Finally, there is one other key aspect of managing and staying in a reciprocal rhythm with *Remarkable* bosses on driving results. This involves signaling them when people are confusing activity with results. Even when strategic priorities and roles have been clarified, human nature is such that people are more often stuck in old patterns than aligned with change and/ or maintaining momentum. If this is not signaled early, if adjustments don't get made, if priorities are not restated, if deadlines are not reinforced – entropy can take hold and seriously impede progress.

Example of Confusing Activity and Results

When Paula, a Senior Vice President, became head of a global business unit, team members complained of stress, fatigue, and of how their efforts were underappreciated. Contrary to this prevailing view, she found that while they were all busy, they were not focused on the right priorities and they lacked a sufficient sense of urgency. She also discovered serious talent gaps in the team. Rather than making the necessary staff changes to achieve the steep business goals set by the President of the division, Paula tried to compensate for poor performers. She also failed to call out the others who were preoccupied with less than value-added tasks. Overwhelmed by the demands of her new role, cascading business problems, and tension with her boss, Paula became mired in the self-limiting habit of compensating for others and ultimately failed in her role.

Managing People

Even *Remarkable* bosses make mistakes on people – bad hires, unwarranted promotions, ill-founded succession decisions. Helping bosses make sound people decisions is one of the most reciprocal "assists" a direct report can provide. Managing bosses well in this dimension of leadership prevents significant problems later, and can accelerate positive team outcomes in the short-term.

One tool for making sound people decisions is the Three-Legged Stool (Table 6.1). Specifically, good staffing decisions pivot on considering three criteria *equally* (1) pedigree (technical/functional/business knowledge), (2) relevant experience, and (3) behavioral "fit" with the organization. Scrutiny of pedigree and experience pose less difficulty than the assessment of the behavior fit factor. However, most ill-fated hires happen because of bad "fit" – but screening for the highly subjective criterion of "fit" continues as a major challenge (Wasylyshyn 2010).

Direct reports who are in reciprocal mode with their bosses on people decisions can go the extra distance by informing bosses about what they might not be seeing in a recruitment scenario, for example. Further, *Remarkable* bosses must sometimes be saved from the seduction of a candidate's technical and experiential credentials – to the exclusion of adequate scrutiny of the behavior fit factor. Using questions based on the four dimensions of emotional intelligence can be a useful adjunct to any hiring process. See this tool in Appendix D.

There are three other potential lessons for helping bosses manage others effectively. The first is making certain that they pay adequate attention to the assimilation or on-boarding of newly hired people. At minimum, a key member of the boss's team serves as a "culture guide" to new hires. The culture guide ensures that new employees are briefed on the behavior norms of the company, receive clues about how to work well with the boss, learn about key processes, get introduced to others, and are given early feedback by the boss.

Table 6.1 The three-legged stool: a model for making sound staffing decisions[a]

Pedigree	Experience	Behavior
To include:	To include:	To include:
• Education – degrees	• Work history	• Emotional intelligence (self awareness, self control, attunement to others, loyal relationships)
• Schools attended	• Special assignments	• "Fit" with company
• Technical training	• Managerial skill	• Leadership style
• Certifications	• Leadership skill	• Harmony with boss and other key stakeholders
• Research grants	• Industry knowledge	• Attitude
• Mentors	• Global experience	• Aspirations
• Continuing education	• Cultural awareness	• Willingness to learn
• Publications	• Management training	• Flexibility
		• Interpersonal skill

[a]Sound staffing decisions are based on an equal emphasis on each of the three-legged stool factors: pedigree, experience, and behavior

Second, in addition to ensuring bosses make good hiring decisions, direct reports can serve as "talent scouts." In this mode, they are focused on assembling a team of "A" players and remain mindful of deepening the bench strength in their bosses' organizations. They do this by identifying high-potential people both inside and outside the company – and helping recruit them to teams if possible.

Third, since *Remarkable* bosses are not immune to subjective feelings about people who report to them – particularly those with whom they have had longstanding relationships – they can benefit from others providing objective talent appraisals of such employees. These appraisals must be specific and fact-based. In the ideal, they should also include ideas for other roles a "fond favorite" of the boss might fill in the organization if they really don't have the ability to handle their current roles.

See Appendix E for a tool to pinpoint the comparative effectiveness of team members. This is based on a two-factor assessment (1) **R** – delivering results (the *what*) and (2) **B** – behavior fit in the team (the *how*).

Executive Credibility

As credible as *Remarkable* leaders typically are the pressure, speed, and complexity of their responsibilities can foster behavioral lapses. This is when direct reports can help manage bosses in ways that minimize the risk of potentially serious credibility gaps. Three Cs (as discussed in Chap. 2) warrant particular attention – communication, consistency, and courage. Reciprocal direct reports will muster their own courage and manage bosses well – in fact, will provide them an invaluable service – by finding ways to give candid feedback in these three areas.

Communication: It's not just what bosses say – it's the combination of their verbals (content) and their nonverbals (facial expression, hand motions, posture) that makes communication either an important asset or a detraction in the repertoire of a senior executive. Communicating the wrong message is an obvious problem. Communicating the right message but doing it flatly or without the necessary non-verbal emphasis is a lost opportunity to motivate or otherwise influence an audience. Giving bosses direct feedback about their *communication combination* of verbals and nonverbals is another way to influence their being maximally effective. Further, in organizations where a boss's "team" is geographically dispersed, a reciprocal direct report will stay attuned to communication needs throughout the organization and signal the boss when it's time for a "live" appearance.

Example of Strong *Communication Combination*

As the new President of a global R&D function in the pharmaceutical industry, Mark was challenged by how to reach the thousands of employees in this organization. He needed to communicate strategy, build alignment, and stimulate renewed enthusiasm and rigor in a culture that was weighed down by the force of its limiting habits. Initial global webcasts had been helpful but Mark could come across as wooden and his passion and certainty about the path forward were eroded by his reading scripts. Ultimately, he took the advice of close advisors and opted for the communication intimacy of regional town hall meetings. He sparkled in these fora and, thus, was able to advance progress on critical business objectives.

Consistency: As consistent as *Remarkable* leaders are generally, they can falter or at least be perceived as behaving inconsistently because the axiom that *reality is perception* predominates in business settings. Under relentless scrutiny, the leader's slightest appearance of inconsistency as related to a strategic decision or objective, for example, can be seized upon and cascade through the organization in waves of confusion – or handy defensiveness against the change that a leader may be trying to effect. The reciprocal direct report is vigilant about perceived inconsistencies and signals the boss accordingly. It is not unusual for the boss to resist this feedback at first. However, the reciprocal direct report will remain dogged about finding ways to deliver necessary feedback persuasively well.

— Example of Executive Consistency Problem —

On the surface, Henry was a charming and clever executive who ran a key area in the supply chain of a global manufacturing company. A classic example of "managing up" well, his direct reports often struggled with his harsh and critical nature, indecisiveness, vagueness, and volatility. Rarely satisfied, he made excessive demands of others especially when he was scheduled to present before senior management. His tendency to change course from one day to the next produced frequent "fire drills" that wasted time and spawned great resentment within his leadership team.

When he noticed that several people in his organization were benefitting from feedback by an external consultant, he asked her if she would provide feedback to him on his leadership style. Trying to seize upon this opportunity to influence at least some adjustment in his leadership behavior, his subordinates were fully candid with the consultant. During Henry's feedback meeting with her, he became increasingly agitated and could not be engaged in development planning. In a subsequent meeting with his team, he said of his feedback, "There were strong points about my ineffectiveness as a leader but I know you didn't mean this. You need to take a hard look at yourselves and what more you can do to support me better."

Courage: *Remarkable* leaders are distinguished by their courage. They relish leading and are willing to speak out, stand alone, influence open debate, probe unexpressed views, and leverage resident wisdom within their companies. They also have the courage to confront anything that might delay or deter business success. This includes poor performers, company "sacred cows," wrong-headed decisions (including their own), and outdated policies and/or processes. Courageous bosses are both a company treasure and a potential liability if they are not as tuned into organizational dynamics as they need to be. Herein lies another opportunity for reciprocal direct reports to manage their courageous bosses. This requires deft truth-telling and making practical suggestions about how bosses might navigate organization dynamics more effectively.

Example of Courageous
————————— Leadership Gone Awry —————————

The top Human Resources executive in the largest division of a global pharmaceutical company, Ted was known for his willingness to speak out on behalf of the company "doing the right thing." In the wake of natural disasters such as the Katrina hurricane and the earthquake in Haiti, he implored corporate executives to donate significant resources to victims' relief. From a public relations perspective, this had enormous positive effects for the corporation.

Equally outspoken on executive character, Ted often provided unvarnished feedback to his boss, the President of this division, about behavior that was perceived as lacking in integrity, short on empathy for others' concerns, and low on authenticity. While his courageous truth-telling often hit the mark, it lacked finesse and was not always as balanced as it might have been with comments about the boss's effectiveness as a leader. Weary of Ted's "harangues," the boss eventually took steps to remove Ted from the organization.

The Merging of Emotional (EQ) and Social Intelligence (SQ)

The emergence of the concept of emotional intelligence – commonly referred to in business as EQ – represented a major step forward in recognizing the critical importance of the behavioral *how* dimension in leadership. This was popularized by psychologist, Goleman (1996, 1998), who highlighted the role of emotions in effective leadership. His research, as well as that of others including Brienza and Cavallo (2005) and Druskat and Wolff (2001), established EQ as a leadership essential for business executives (see Table 1.2).

A developable capability, even Jack "neutron" Welch, former Chairman and CEO of GE, had by the end of his career emphasized the importance of EQ in leadership. In his words, "No doubt emotional intelligence is more rare than book smarts, but my experience says it is actually *more* important in the making of a leader. You just can't ignore it."(2004, p. A14).

Further, Goleman et al. (2002) highlighted the importance of *empathic resonance* if one is to be an effective leader. In their words, "The fundamental task of leaders is to prime good feeling in those they lead. That occurs when a leader creates resonance – a reservoir of positivity that frees the best in people. At its root, then, the primal job of leadership is emotional" (p. ix).

While the concept of emotional intelligence continues to hold its place in leadership development initiatives and coaching practice, research in the field of social neuroscience – the study of what happens in the brain when people interact – further informs our understanding of successful leadership. Referring to this as social intelligence, Goleman and Boyatzis (2008) maintain, "The salient discovery is that certain things leaders do – specifically, exhibit empathy and become attuned to others' moods – literally affect both their own brain chemistry and that of their followers ... We believe that great leaders are those whose behavior powerfully leverages the system of brain interconnectedness" (p. 2).

Social intelligence (SQ) is measured on the basis of seven social intelligence qualities – empathy, attunement, organizational awareness, influence, developing others, inspiration, and teamwork. These qualities are all behaviorally based further reinforcing the critical importance of the *how* dimension of leadership.

Direct reports who are in reciprocal relationships with their *Remarkable* bosses will want to find ways to help them leverage this differentiating leadership capability. The following seven questions – aligned with EQ and the seven social intelligence qualities cited above – should prove a useful tool in doing so.

Exercise

───── **Leveraging Combined EQ and SQ** ─────

*R*ead the questions in these seven areas and identify potential ways *you could help your Remarkable boss leverage his/her combination of EQ and SQ.*

- Empathy – Am I signaling my boss so he/she is sufficiently responsive to the concerns of people on our team?
- Attunement – How can I ensure that my boss meets our major customers – both internal and external – where they need to be met?
- Organizational awareness – Is my boss as aware of organization dynamics as he/she needs to be? If not, what am I going to do to ensure this?

- Influence – What more can I do to assist my boss in being as persuasive and influential as he/she needs to be especially in terms of advancing our top objectives?
- Developing others – How can I aid my boss in retaining and developing our top talent and in raising the bar on talent management issues in general?
- Inspiration – Have I done all I could to convey the examples of success and commitment in our organization that my boss can use to inspire our best collective efforts going forward? Have I given feedback about the good job he/she does in instilling hope about the future here?
- Teamwork – Have I conveyed my best thoughts about how our team could be even more effective than it already is?

Example of Merged EQ and SQ

In his book the ART of LEADERSHIP, Max DePree tells a poignant – and from a leadership perspective – most revealing story about his grandfather, the founder of Herman Miller. Some days after the millwright of the firm died, DePree's grandfather went to pay his respects to the millwright's widow. As they conversed, the wife mentioned that her husband had written poetry and the elder DePree asked if he could read some of the poems. After doing so, he said to the widow that he could not be sure if her husband was a millwright who happened to write poetry or a poet who happened to be a millwright.

There's a Buddhist saying about when the student is ready, the teacher arrives. One of the most significant factors that continues to propel the applicability of emotional and social intelligence in the work place is globalization. In emerging markets – particularly Asia – management styles tend to be more relationship-based than in North America (Triandis 1993). Increasingly, business leaders have had to become more attuned to the relationship subtleties and nuances of doing business with leaders and other key stakeholders in these emerging markets.

Remarkable bosses and the people who report to them *must* stay in an ongoing and deepening dialog about their respective experiences and apply these insights about how to do business and win in these emerging markets.

Behavior Observations of *Remarkable* Leaders: Three Clues for Managing Them

Of all the many behavioral assets of *Remarkable* leaders, there are three interrelated behaviors that I consider especially noteworthy: boldness, enterprise-wide thinking, and empowerment. The *Remarkable* business executives whom I've known all possessed their own brand of taking bold action, making decisions based on both panoramic and ground-level views of the entire organization, and leading through empowered teams populated by gifted people.

Boldness

In conversations with global CEOs, I often asked what they considered to be the most critical behavioral requirement of a C-level leader. The most frequent answers always involved some variant of *bold* or *daring*. This serves as the first important behavioral clue for managing *Remarkable* leaders well.

Direct reports who are on solid reciprocal ground with their bosses have the opportunity to take their own bold actions, as well as to influence the bold actions of their bosses.

Exercise

Managing a *Remarkable* Boss's
———— Bold Actions ————

Test yourself on the extent to which you can be relied on by your boss for the following:

- Ensuring that my boss's passion and excitement about a bold action does not overwhelm having sufficient facts, analyses, and the consideration of all other relevant factors
- Giving a timely signal to my boss when a particular bold move seems warranted
- Playing an ambassadorial role down into the organization about the rightness of a bold move – especially when there may be significant resistance in the organization
- Giving the boss enthusiastic recognition of bold steps that paid off

- Serving as an early and trusted warning signal when a bold move starts looking bad
- Helping to rally and calm the troops before a troubled bold mission is aborted prematurely
- Helping capture the "lessons learned" from a bold mission that went down, storing these lessons for future use, and ensuring that the boss remembers them when he/she needs to, i.e., before putting the next bold move into motion

---

Enterprise-Wide Thinking

The second significant behavioral clue for managing *Remarkable* bosses is enterprise-wide thinking. While this term may elicit varying connotations, in this context, it is used to refer to leadership behavior that is based on a holistic view of a business organization. Invariably, this is a view that is focused on decisions and other actions that will help create sustainable success for the future. In this sense, these leaders are driving forces of change. This view integrates strategic, people, and organizational dynamics considerations.

Given the strong cognitive and analytical capabilities of *Remarkable* leaders, they are readily able to see patterns and connect-the-dots to produce elegant and timely solutions for enterprise-wide challenges. A host of behavioral assets including their active engagement with internal and external stakeholders, their ability for conceptual reasoning, futuristic orientation, and disciplined approach further equip them for the demands of the integrated problem-solving characteristic of sound enterprise-wide thinking.

Further, the constructive people management sensibilities of *Remarkable* leaders coupled with their healthy (unneurotic) personalities, and strong emotional intelligence further reinforce the strength of their enterprise-wide observations and decision-making.

List of Enterprise-Wide Thinking Behaviors of Remarkable Leaders[5]

- Takes a holistic view when making business decisions – a view that includes social, economic, and environmental factors, as well as conventional customer, market, and competition factors.
- Takes a holistic, and unselfish, view when making people decisions – a view that includes needs of the business, team dynamics, organizational considerations, as well as individual employee learning and development.

- Integrates business strategies, organization leadership and capabilities, organization needs, and expectations into an effective management system that yields innovative solutions for customers, shareholders, and employees.
- Allocates resources in a manner that supports both short-term needs and longer-term investments.
- Makes adjustments in organization structure to better support business priorities.
- Influences the thinking of more senior leaders to ensure a holistic perspective on key business issues and/or decisions.
- Ensures that all levels within the organization have a shared understanding of and commitment to accomplishing broader initiatives.
- Strives to achieve superior and sustainable organization performance that exceeds current challenges and addresses expectations for the future.

Exercise

Questions for increasing the enterprise-wide ——— behavior of a *Remarkable* boss ———

With enterprise-wide thinking front of mind, consider these questions as a guide or template for stimulating ideas about how you might manage a *Remarkable* boss to be even more effective in terms of his/her enterprise-wide behavior.

- What more can I do to arm my boss with all the internal and external information he/she needs for upcoming business decisions? Is there additional customer, market, and/or competitor information that I could provide? Are there social, economic, and/or environmental issues that he/she may not be aware of?
- Am I resisting employee moves my boss has suggested because of my selfish need to retain certain people in their current positions?
- Are there suggestions that I could make about exporting talent from my organization that would serve them and the overall business as well?
- Am I willing to take a risk and import certain people into my organization – people whom I may not see as fully ready for certain roles but who nevertheless have potential?
- Am I willing to give up financial and people resources, i.e., have them shifted to other parts of the organization where they are needed to support more urgent business priorities?

- Are there changes in organization structure that would better support the current strategy but I am resisting this because I think it would erode my power base?
- When was the last time I steppcd up to my ambassadorial role as a manager and ensured that there was sufficient clarity throughout the organization regarding my boss's strategy, key objectives, accountabilities, and timelines?
- When my boss is struggling with senior management to position his/her view on a particular issue, how willing am I to provide back-up and/or leverage relationships I have that might prove helpful?
- Do I think about the business holistically or do I stay hunkered down in my silo trying to keep up with current objectives? If I were to be more intentional about assuming a holistic view, what are the few most value-added steps I could take right now? What's getting in the way of my taking these steps?
- As I look to the future, what's the one BIG goal I could set and ensure achievement of that would be meaningful for my team and helpful to my boss's overall view of the enterprise for the next year?

Empowerment

The third significant behavioral clue for managing *Remarkable* bosses well is *empowerment* – specifically, their deeply held belief about the strength of leading through empowered teams. By the time *Remarkable* leaders have reached officer-level responsibility (Vice President), they have had their share of bosses. Those experiences – good and bad – coupled with their abilities to trust, prioritize the development of talented others, and convey their own wisdom and experiences – influence their natural affinity for an empowered leadership model.

Aside from their personal beliefs about effective leadership, this model makes sense in a business climate where organizations have become increasingly flatter and leaner. Further, other relevant developments to include globalization, geographically dispersed teams, the information technology explosion, strategic alliances, and the increase in the number of mergers and acquisitions have taken hold. An empowering leadership style is also an effective response to rapidly shifting workplace dynamics that include younger employees managing those older than they, two-career couples, greater gender mixed and ethnically diverse teams, and increasing numbers of employees working virtually from all parts of the planet.

The list of behaviors central in *Remarkable* executives' empowering leadership is long – and admirable. Below is a representative look at these behaviors.

List of Empowering Behaviors of *Remarkable* Leaders

- Appetite for innovative ideas
- Celebrates triumphs with overt praise and/or awards
- Challenges employees with rewarding tasks
- Communicates a compelling vision that inspires people because it indicates their place in it
- Desire to encourage/guide others
- Encourages the growth and self-actualization of others
- Encourages risk-taking
- Favors teaching/coaching over harsh criticism or judging
- Gives people permission to fail and time to learn in the wake of mistakes
- Grooms potential successors
- Leverages diversity of people and ideas
- Listens, listens always listens well
- Makes work fun
- Minimizes dependence of employees on the boss
- Orchestrates success experiences that make employees feel more competent
- Promotes collaborative team-based leadership
- Provides motivational support
- Receptive to challenges and others' ideas
- Relishes change – is flexible and adaptive in the face of it
- Shares information and resources
- Trusts in the skills, intentions, and decision-making ability of others
- Urges new and better ways of doing things
- Willingness to share power
- World class delegator committed to *not* being a bottleneck

Exercise

Questions for increasing the empowerment behaviors of a *Remarkable* boss

With these empowering leadership behaviors front-of-mind, consider the following questions as a template for guiding how you might manage a *Remarkable* boss and, in doing so, help him/her be even more effective.

- Have I been as forthcoming as I could be in expressing my potentially innovative ideas?
- Do I signal the boss about people in the team when they need more encouragement or motivational support from him/her?
- Are there decisions that the team could be making but we keep getting stalled or hung up on certain issues? If so, what can I get from the boss that would help us move forward?
- When the boss is in fact a bottleneck, what do I do to address this?
- What can I do to aid my boss in the grooming of his/her best successor?
- Do I make sure to let my boss know when certain people and/or parts of the organization would benefit from some praise, or when specific awards seem warranted?
- Am I explicit enough with my boss about development opportunities for myself or others that would really contribute to both individual growth and team effectiveness?
- When I know my peers are being overly dependent on our boss, do I call them out on it and urge our taking better advantage of the empowerment we've been given?
- When we need to learn more from the boss, especially when something hasn't gone well, do I pursue and/or help create the opportunity for that teaching/coaching to occur?
- When I recognize better ways to do things, what do I do to engage my boss in our implementing change?
- When there's a disconnect between what the boss thinks is going on in the team and what I know to be true – especially when things are not going well – what do I do to promote a better working rhythm or to reach out for help to get things back on track?
- What more can I do to leverage the resident wisdom that the boss has placed in the team, i.e., fully using the talents and experiences of others?
- What more do I need to do to carry the boss's vision down through the organization and to excite others about how our committed efforts will contribute to the success of the company?
- How can I join in my boss's efforts to ensure that work is fun?

To conclude, the over-arching, unexpected lesson about managing *Remarkable* bosses is the *power of reciprocity* – forming strong reciprocal relationships with them. Akin to strong marriages, in these reciprocal relationships, each partner is simultaneously fully committed to the other – as well as to his/her own growth and self-actualization. Challenges, accomplishments, disappointments, and failures are shared equally – and are mined for sustained learning. Traditional leadership competencies (strategic thinking, driving results, people management, and executive credibility) are merged with essential leadership behaviors (emotional intelligence plus social intelligence, boldness, enterprise-thinking, and empowerment). Through the power of reciprocal commitments, bosses apply these competencies and behaviors – and their direct reports are free to discover and apply their own versions of these competencies and behaviors. In the end, all parties thrive and evolve: bosses, their subordinates, and the business organizations they serve.

LESSON PLAN for MANAGING
a *REMARKABLE BOSS*

BUILD A RECIPROCAL RELATIONSHIP WITH BOSS
Replace "What's in it for me?" with "What's in it for us?"
BRAND YOUR STRATEGIC POTENTIAL
Be intentional about stretching a boss's strategic thinking, and revealing yours.
TRANSCEND THE TACTICAL
Conquer your inner "doing demon." Define yourself more by your ideas and what you can influence versus merely by task completion.
BE AN AMBASSADOR
Reinforce the boss's strategy through your interactions with others in the organization. Help ensure alignment and commitment to achieving strategic objectives.
ACCELERATE RESULTS
Call people out on the difference between "being busy" and actually "getting results." Influence the use of ART-ful delegation.
HELP GET RIGHT PEOPLE IN RIGHT ROLES
Ensure your boss puts an "A" team in place, avoids retaining mediocre team members, and makes the tough people decisions quickly. Ensure effective assimilation of new managers.
BE A TALENT SCOUT
Stay on the alert for top talent. Help recruit great people from both within and outside the organization.
BE A TRUTH TELLER
Insight is cheap unless you use it. Say what you see especially in terms of your boss's (1) communication effectiveness, (2) consistency (mouth and feet match), and (3) courage to do the hard and right things.
DEVELOP YOUR COMBINED EQ and SQ
Know yourself – what you feel, as well as what you know. Use this emotional awareness as a tool in partnering with your boss to connect to people in ways that promote stellar results.
BE AN ENTERPRISE PLAYER
Get out of your silo. Think holistically. Work interdisciplinarily. Convey what you know generously. Believe that your collaborative work with others will often exceed what you could accomplish alone.
LEVERAGE EMPOWERMENT
Challenge yourself and others to leverage the empowerment your boss has given.

End Notes

[1] In this context, pleasing bosses is seen as very much a part of managing them well.

[2] While the life history and other psychological data presented in Chap. 2 were helpful in describing this leadership type, the leadership competency, EQ, and behavioral observation data yield the most accessible and pragmatic guidance regarding ways to manage them.

[3] Even when you do not connect with your boss on strategy discussion and/or planning initially, if you aspire to bigger roles in the organization, you should persist in these efforts because you need to build your brand as someone with strategic potential. In corporate talent review processes, strategic thinking is the sine qua non for inclusion on the top "high potential" list. These are individuals who warrant special development opportunities, as well as level promotions and concomitant increases in compensation. If, despite your continued efforts, you still do not get traction with your boss in discussing issues at a strategic level, then seek a mentoring relationship with someone higher in the company and/or become involved in special projects or task forces that will give you an opportunity to apply your strategic capability.

[4] Social intelligence (SQ) is defined as "… a set of interpersonal competencies built on specific neural circuits (and related endocrine systems) that inspire others to be effective" (Goleman and Boyatzis 2008, p. 74).

[5] In this context the author is focused on executives in C-level roles but extrapolations can be made to mid level managerial leaders.

Managing a *Perilous* Boss

> *The best leaders act courageously but keep their egos under control knowing that they do not own the truth. They must seek the truth through respectful and trusting partnerships with others.*
>
> Pierre Brondeau
> Chairman and CEO, FMC

Perilous leaders can be too arrogant, dominant, suspicious, and/or chameleon to form respectful and trusting partnerships that thrive over time. Chronic discontent – or what I call "unrequited work" – diminishes their tolerance for the truth-seeking Pierre Brondeau, an exceptionally *Remarkable* leader, urges in the quote that opens this chapter (personal communication, February 14, 2010). Such truth-seeking necessitates the suspension of one's ego and a willingness to be vulnerable. However, vulnerability exacerbates discontent and so it is fiercely defended against by most *Perilous* business executives.

The cartoon here evokes another important point about *Perilous* leaders – the presence of long-standing psychological issues related to childhood development factors described in Chap. 3. These difficulties include variable self-esteem and emotional immaturity that can compromise their effectiveness as leaders.

K.M. Wasylyshyn, *Behind the Executive Door: Unexpected Lessons for Managing Your Boss and Career*, DOI 10.1007/978-1-4614-0376-0_7,
© Karol M. Wasylyshyn 2012

Cartoon by Jennifer Berman, 1991 - Pocket books/Simon & Schuster

Despite their many talents and accomplishments, there is an underlying belief that they could have done more, been more, striven for more, and thus they remain psychologically checkmated in "unrequited work." As indicated in Chap. 3, the word "unrequited" in this context is used to describe the lack of contentment with one's work-related achievements. This sense of "unrequited work" can fuel chronic feelings of career frustration and disappointment. In extreme cases, a pervasive feeling of unrequited work can lead to a major depression.

Major Lesson for Managing a *Perilous* Boss: Reducing the Sense of "Unrequited Work"

The effective management of a *Perilous* boss – or avoiding being one – hinges on this: the ability to reduce that boss's sense of "unrequited work." This means that as a direct report, you are caring and generous, and you will seize opportunities to bolster your boss's pride and work-related contentment. You will strive to influence a different reality for your *Perilous* boss. In this reality, his/her self-limiting thoughts, harsh self-criticism, and doubts or shame have been swept off the table by your efforts to help him/her do so. These negative factors have been replaced by nutritious helpings of highlighted strengths and accomplishments – accomplishments that they are encouraged to digest and savor fully as their own. In this reality, the danger of indigestion or food poisoning is nil. The likelihood of healthy and strong leadership is magnified because direct reports are committed to underscoring the reasons why this is possible.

Through these efforts to reduce their bosses' feelings of unrequited work, direct reports can be catalytic in helping *Perilous* leaders reach their full potential. Herein lies the most unexpected lesson of managing *Perilous* bosses: their subordinates' selfless and caring acts can match – and even surpass – what these bosses do for them. I propose the potential of reciprocal altruism as a management ideal to influence humanistic and competitive twenty-first century workplace dynamics – but this is a topic for another time.

Example of Reducing a Boss's Sense of Unrequited Work

Raised in an emotionally "cool" home where, in Dave's words, "You had better get things right and get to the top of the class if you wanted an extra cookie in your lunch box," any affection or acknowledgement he received was completely conditional on his academic performance. Even as he began to distinguish himself as a pitcher on his Little League baseball team, his father rarely attended a game maintaining, "Why would I spend an afternoon doing that – you're not going to make a living from it."

After serving in the Vietnam War, he completed a college education and took the first job he could get – reporting for a local newspaper in the Northeast. Eventually, he became a well-respected science reporter, writer, and editor and was hired by a global publishing company in Manhattan. Married by this time with several children, he was haunted by feelings of having compromised his true abilities and settled for work that held little meaning for him but that he needed to do to support his family. After 21 years, he began to drink heavily, his marriage collapsed, and he was close to getting fired.

One of his direct reports, an aspiring young journalist who had become a confidant, began to discuss his circumstances more seriously, all the while reinforcing his past and current accomplishments, as well as conveying the respect others had for his significant capabilities. She also encouraged his pursuit of an entrepreneurial publishing venture that seemed a better fit for his skills and temperament, as well as his creative writing. Within a few years, he had remarried, become financially stable, and began to be published in notable literary journals.

Working for a *Perilous* boss is fraught with numerous difficulties. Their behavior can be erratic, confusing, rigidly demanding, and lacking in appreciation. Much of this behavior is a projection of their inner realities – realities that are frozen, dark, and humorless. But at the same time, they are capable of being as effective as *Remarkable* leaders; hence, efforts invested in helping them get there can be rewarding for both those willing to offer assistance, as well as for the leaders who can receive it.[1]

The remainder of this chapter focuses on practical ways to manage *Perilous* bosses – bosses who would likely be receptive to such efforts. This content is guided by the leadership competencies, emotional intelligence, and behavioral observations of *Perilous* leaders as provided in Chap. 3.

Leadership Competencies

Strategy

While *Perilous* leaders possess the intellectual horsepower and business acumen to do well with strategy, this is not always the case. As indicated in Chap. 3, there are issues related to trust, wanting to keep their options open, competitiveness, a preference for thinking on their own, and independent decision-making that can erode their effectiveness on this leadership competency. Any one or combination of these issues can sabotage the likelihood of their getting strategic alignment and maintaining execution on core strategic objectives. These inevitabilities can trigger *Perilous* leaders' worse behaviors, including giving angry directives, petulant withdrawal, and even frustrated capitulation to others' strategic thoughts – which may not be as well founded as their own.

Direct reports who wish to manage, i.e., elicit the best strategic behavior of their *Perilous* bosses, can begin with the fundamental first step of drawing them into that type of conversation. This will likely happen best in a regularly scheduled face-to-face meeting with the boss – one in which the direct report comes prepared with germane and potentially useful thoughts about the business or functional area that the boss is leading. If this goes well, a possible second step could be adding "strategy" to team meeting agendas. The goal is for the boss to have incrementally positive experiences of discussing strategic issues with his/her subordinates – experiences that contribute to the overall quality of strategic planning, decision-making, and execution.

Anyone who wants to do a better job of managing a *Perilous* boss on strategy must be both tactful and nimble: tactful enough to not seem critical or competitive, nimble enough to engage the boss quickly – and meaningfully – in

Example of Influencing a *Perilous* Boss's
——————— Strategic Thinking ———————

Kathryn was charged with creating a new group of services for a growing division of a regional consulting firm. As a partner in the firm, she had considerable customer interface and a business background that surpassed that of her direct reports. She had been struggling in her own thoughts with the new services objective for several months when one of her subordinates suggested she hold an off-site meeting during which they include this topic on the agenda. Kathryn agreed.

Her direct reports came well prepared for the strategy part of the agenda having polled clients on their needs and completed an analysis of services being offered by competing firms. The meeting was an overall success, and within months, Kathryn's group launched two new services that did well and served as a prelude to additional others.

---

this objective. Further, efforts to influence a boss and help manage, if you will, his/her best strategic behavior will be rewarded when direct reports:

- Do their homework – as did Kathryn's team in the above example
- Orchestrate successive substantive conversations that foster a new pattern related to the discussion of strategic issues
- Influence an atmosphere of transparency, i.e., sharing information, engaging in open brainstorming, importing pearls of strategic input from other companies, and conveying the team's collaborative intention, thus building the boss's trust and engagement

Driving Results

Most *Perilous* leaders stake their reputations completely on what they deliver, and their moods rise and fall in accordance with their results. For some, their innermost fear – irrational as it may be – is that they "will be history" if they do not continue to deliver certain quarter-by-quarter results. The stress of this is obvious. Less obvious, perhaps, is the fact that embedded in this formulation of their leadership identity is at least some awareness that there is not a lot more to commend them as leaders, i.e., not a lot more beyond their specific results. This narrow depiction of themselves as leaders is one of their harshest and most self-limiting thoughts. It is at the core of their sense of unrequited work.

- HOPE – Leaders instill hope in people by engaging in frequent and clear communication regarding the reasons why employees should feel inspired and excited about the future. These messages emphasize strength of the strategic direction, specificity of objectives and realistic timelines, the effectiveness of the company's growth/success, robustness of the culture, strength of the leadership and the implications of these growth, success, culture, and leadership factors for employees' individual success and work-related aspirations.

- ACKNOWLEDGEMENT – Public comments about what's working well in the organization. Leaders capitalize on genuine opportunities to affirm employees' good work, to reward well, to celebrate success, to build on aspects of the culture that ensure momentum, timely results, and competitive advantage.

- TRUTH-TELLING – Stating reality as it truly *is*. Leaders present an accurate picture of what's going on currently. They have the courage to confront the truth. They are persistently candid about what's *real now* including business results, business problems, business projections, and people performance

IN TOUGH TIMES, THE BEST LEADERS MAKE PERSPECTIVE -- *by emphasizing* hope. Acknowledgement and Truth-telling are essential but they must not overwhelm hope i.e., statements about and encouragement toward a successful future.

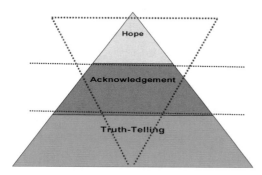

Fig. 7.1 Perspective-making – a fundamental leadership responsibility

It follows then that when results are falling short of projections, these leaders need special attention – or "management" from those around them lest they spiral down and make things intensely miserable for others, as well as for themselves. One of the best "managing" steps direct reports can take in times like these is to help bosses maintain perspective. Based on this objective and pragmatic approach (see Fig. 7.1), there are four key questions that can help focus the leader's attention. See below.

Perspective-Making as a Tool for Managing the Fears of a *Perilous* Boss*

- Truth-telling – What are the true facts about the current situation?
- Acknowledgment – What is it about our strategy, people, organization, and other factors that's working now?
- Pragmatic action – How can I use what's working to respond to the truth of the current situation? If I really don't have what I need now, what do I need to do to get it?
- Hope – What do I need to do as a leader to weave together the truth of our current situation and what we can assemble to respond to the issue(s) in a way that restores hope in the organization?

*When all else fails, tell your boss that FEAR is an acronym for: False Evidence Appearing Real.

When *Perilous* bosses are helped (managed) to maintain perspective, they usually calm down enough to see things clearly, clarify ambiguity, and channel their business acumen and intellectual and psychic energies toward achieving the results they need. If there's no way those results can be forthcoming, the exercise/discipline of making perspective can be grounding enough to help them manage and/or readjust the expectations of *their* bosses.

Example of Using Perspective-Making to Ease a *Perilous* Boss's Concerns

While CEO success metrics in charitable nonprofit organizations differ from those of for-profit entities, the pressure on these leaders to "deliver" certain results to key stakeholders is comparable. In the regional chapter of a national volunteer-based organization, a leader had assumed the total burden for achieving an aggressive capital campaign goal. As the economy worsened, corporations curbed their charitable giving, foundation support faded, and individual donors dropped away, she became increasingly pessimistic, judgmental of staff, and self-critical.

Members of her executive team persuaded her to hold an off-site retreat facilitated by an outside consultant known to the organization. Having been well briefed by both the CEO and members of her leadership team, the consultant helped the CEO arrive at a clearer perspective on the issues. A realistic and revitalized plan about how to ride the waves of fierce economic currents at the time was also created. Further, the staff ensured that this plan remained a guiding document, i.e., the centerpiece of their ongoing efforts to complete the capital campaign.

Managing People

Perilous leaders can have numerous problems on this leadership competency, including (1) making bad hires, (2) not assimilating new hires well, (3) failing to give candid and frequent feedback, (4) limited focus on employee development, and (5) insufficient attention to providing rewards and psychological paychecks.[2] These issues can be compounded by others that further diminish the overall effectiveness of *Perilous* bosses. These include their lack of clarity regarding roles, accountabilities, deadlines, and resources.

Like *Remarkable* leaders, these leaders are vulnerable for making bad people decisions. Because effective hiring is more of an art than a science, it continues as an issue of some magnitude for most organizations. In the current job market, it is probably less about available talent than it is about the "fit" of a person with the culture of the hiring organization. I recently wrote, "Most hiring managers know how to assess a candidate's technical qualifications and relevant work experience. However, successful recruitment ... requires the scrutiny of how people work, manage, and lead. This subjective behavior dimension is much more difficult to assess with certainty, and it is often the major factor in a poor hiring decision" (Wasylyshyn 2010, p. 19).

Some companies hire licensed psychologists to conduct psychological assessments focused on the behavioral "fit" of individuals with their organization cultures. Others, for whom testing might not be culturally syntonic, rely on the behavior screening skill of their HR professionals. Some savvy organizations use a combination of behavior event interviewing (BEI) and questions based on the four dimensions of emotional intelligence (EQ) to screen for the behavior "fit" factor. See Appendix D for examples of such questions.

When making bad hires has been an issue for *Perilous* leaders, direct reports can manage them by inserting steps into the hiring process that impose more scrutiny of candidates' behavior "fit." Using EQ-informed interview questions is an example of such a step.

Perilous leaders are vulnerable for making bad hires for an array of reasons. Some are arrogant (*I know what I'm looking for and can spot it*). With others, their own variable EQ can interfere with their being sufficiently attuned to critical candidate behavioral signals in interview situations. Still, others get overly fixated on recruiting high-pedigree candidates and the challenge of seducing gifted candidates into their organizations (*He may not be an exact fit for us but his background is so impressive, I have to have him and I know I can persuade him to join us*).

——— Example of a Recruitment Gone Bad ———

A seasoned Human Resources professional who specialized in leadership development, Bill had worked for a prestigious Fortune 100 company before he accepted the top HR role in the most profitable division of another global company. Despite his reservations about not being a fully qualified HR generalist, he was charmed by his prospective boss and assured by both his predecessor who was retiring and the boss that the "nuts and bolts" demands of the role were minimal compared to the organization's need for what Bill had to offer.

Without a sufficient assimilation process, adrift in an alpha male culture, and finding it difficult to establish rapport with a boss who proved to be enigmatic and a lot less charismatic and supportive than he was in the hiring phase, Bill faltered from the outset. Being a strong introvert didn't help matters, so it was difficult for him to get traction with even his functional direct reports who resented his lack of generalist HR background. In less than a year, Bill left the company.

Like the boss who hired Bill, many *Perilous* leaders can have difficulty in forming and motivating high-performance teams. Their fundamental issues with trust, idiosyncratic behavior, impatience, frustration, and lack of clarity regarding roles, accountabilities, priorities, and a host of other issues makes working for them, in the words of one vice president, "More like something to endure than to enjoy."

Further, various problems with *Perilous* leaders providing feedback also decrease their effectiveness in managing others on an individual or team basis. Lacking in EQ, these leaders can be overly blunt or even whiplash people between accepting and rejecting comments and behavior. (See *Stranded* in Chap. 9 for a metaphorical example of this.) Others are so indirect and/or inconsistent that people are never quite certain where they stand. And still other *Perilous* leaders are not in the habit of providing much feedback at all. Since these leaders also may not place talent development as a priority, high-potential employees, in particular, may have memorable learning experiences with them, but inevitably, they will want to move on into assignments with bosses who are genuinely focused on the development of top talent.

Finally, direct reports are not always confident that their *Perilous* bosses will go-to-bat for them or influence decisions that impact them significantly. For example, they can be disappointed by bosses who won't advocate for their promotions and concomitant pay increases. Further, high-potential managers can feel blocked given limited exposure to senior management because their bosses are more focused on seizing such opportunities for themselves.

Executive Credibility

If it were not for their innate intellectual, analytical problem-solving, and business acumen strengths (or functional expertise for those leaders who are running functions versus being in general management), *Perilous* leaders would probably have many greater problems in this leadership competency area. However, that being said, there are behavioral considerations of note in the areas of communication, consistency, and courage that warrant exploration. These provide particular opportunities for direct reports who are willing to try to manage their bosses in these areas – and in so doing, help them minimize executive credibility issues.

Communication

Regarding communication – especially communication with groups – many *Perilous* leaders would benefit from others' efforts to help them be more attuned to their audiences versus being primarily focused on the content of their remarks.

— Example of "Connecting" Communication —

A *Perilous* leader walked onto an auditorium stage for an all-hands meeting and began by saying, "I have a prepared deck that we can go through together, or I can push that aside and start responding to your comments and questions right now. Which would you prefer?" While this might strike some as a pretty risky move, it proved to be one of the most memorable things this executive (now retired) ever did in his trips to visit employees based in Europe. In short, this was an example of exquisite audience attunement that boosted his executive credibility immeasurably.

Consistency

As described in Chap. 3, the unrequited work dynamic experienced by *Perilous* leaders can foster inconsistent and confusing behavior especially for those reporting to them. While this type of behavior is difficult to manage especially when leaders are not happy with business results, they will be well served, i.e., managed well by subordinates who tactfully point out inconsistencies in directives, for example. Further, pointing out the adverse effects of the leader's sudden mood changes and/or increased expressions of frustration, disappointment, and criticism can also be helpful. Oftentimes, humor can be a handy "management" tool in these circumstances. Specifically, making comments such as:

> Was it something that I said that produced your sudden change in mood today?
> It looks like we missed the goal line again – what do we need to do to adjust?
> You probably think we're one of the worst teams in the industry but we are fearless, so what should we try now?

Example of Providing Timely, Candid Feedback

A t times, a trusted external person can be helpful in providing a boss timely and candid feedback. For example, a management consultant who had an excellent rapport with the Founder/CEO of a technical services firm once conveyed to him that his recent rampage of critical comments had left most of his immediate staff feeling "pounded" and confused. While the CEO half grunted at the consultant, his most severely critical behavior abated. He also provided more clarity regarding his expectations, and the staff was afforded at least temporary relief.

Courage

The combination of feelings of unrequited work, self-absorption, and the stress of disappointing results can seriously diminish the likelihood of *Perilous* leaders behaving courageously. While they are capable of waging powerful and convincing debates on strategy or other issues, they can also disappoint. Further, if they are feeling on slippery ground with their boss, they may be even less inclined than most to take up controversial issues and/or to press for policy changes.

Both peers and direct reports can play a pivotal role in influencing the courageous behavior of *Perilous* leaders. To not do so – especially on key strategic and/or organization-based issues – runs the risk of these leaders, their teams and peers alike losing political capital with senior management. While the issues can vary, one of the most robust tools for managing bosses in this way remains the same: the mirror.

In essence this is a reciprocal courage that necessitates the other holding a mirror up to *Perilous* leaders at a time and in a place where they can look into it fully – and clearly. Ideally, through this clear reflection they are reminded of their successful past acts of courageous leadership, and can be exhorted to act courageously again. Efforts to manage this behavior of *Perilous* leaders should also include (1) the provision of a powerful rationale as to why they must take a certain stand and (2) the promise of any active back-up that may be needed from others.

– Example of a Lack of Courageous Leadership –

As the demands of international travel increased for most members of a Business Manager's team, they requested more flexibility in their work schedules – specifically, the ability to work from home the day before or after extensive travel. A self-proclaimed and proud "workaholic," as was the CEO of the company, this *Perilous* boss refused to take up their request to influence a company policy change. He knew this would infuriate the CEO. Further, at a team meeting, this boss stated that people who expressed concerns about work–family balance lacked ambition. Eventually, his lack of courage and inflexibility on this issue led to a key high-potential team member leaving the company to work for a competitor that supported a "virtual" working model.

The Merging of Emotional Intelligence (EQ) and Social Intelligence (SQ)

Perilous leaders possess variable degrees of EQ and SQ and can be limited in the extent to which they integrate the two for more effective leadership. Therefore, there are myriad opportunities for direct reports to manage them, i.e., influence their greater effectiveness as leaders.

Exercise

Warning Signs of *Perilous* Bosses Who Lack EQ/SQ – and Clues for How to Help Them

Using the four SO SMART® dimensions of EQ, review (1) the warning signs in each dimension that indicate why *Perilous* bosses can benefit from assistance and (2) the boss management clue – or "1–2 combination statements" technique – that can serve as a potentially effective tool for helping them lead with greater EQ/SQ.

SO – Self-Observation

- Warning sign: Lacks an accurate understanding of own strengths and weaknesses.
- *Boss management clue*: Using "1–2 combination statements" in which (1) a boss strength is highlighted – because it made a difference in a specific outcome and (2) a boss weakness is mentioned – because it limited a better outcome.

    1. *Your ability to motivate the team is awe-inspiring like in our staff meeting last month when you described our competitive advantage over other companies in our space and the implications of that for changes in our marketing materials.*

    2. *But you know what, it turned out that we really needed more access to you over the last month, but we couldn't get it, so we sort of flew blind on this and the outcome of the modified marketing materials was just not that great.*

SM – Self-Management

- Warning sign: Inability to control and/or channel both positive and negative emotions effectively.
- *Boss management clue*: Using "1–2 combination statements" to (1) reinforce the use of positive emotion (satisfaction, affirmation, happiness, etc.) and (2) limit the inappropriate use of negative emotion (anger, frustration, impatience, etc.).[3]
  1. *At the CEO Forum, that was fantastic the way you recognized the R&D team on our project. Everyone was really pumped up by that.*
  2. *On the flip side, there are times when your anger and disappointment can get the best of you, and instead of going after specific people in a meeting, it would really be better if you took certain issues behind closed doors. We can see your displeasure coming in meetings, and it just makes people pretty much clam up for the rest of the time.*

A – Attunement to Others

- Warning sign: Not well-attuned to the needs, concerns, ideas of others. Lack of empathy.
- *Boss management clue*: Using "1–2 combination statements" to (1) to reinforce attuned listening and interaction and (2) to increase empathic resonance with others.
  1. *The way you facilitated that meeting with the Regional Vice Presidents was masterful. They got to put all their concerns on the table, and you didn't jump into problem-solving mode before you heard enough about what's really going on in the field.*
  2. *On the other hand, there are times when you're just a speeding train and your sense of urgency overrides the real ability you have to connect to others – that empathic caring that really makes them feel like you're with them and get what they're having to deal with to meet our sales objectives. When you do that, you really motivate people's best efforts; when you don't, they start feeling like cogs in a wheel.*

RT – Relationship Traction

- Warning sign: Relationships are primarily transactional (*This is what I need you to do now*) versus more personal and connected (*We've got some very difficult things to do together but along the way, I'd like to learn more about you and the other parts of your life*).
- *Boss management clue*: Using "1–2 combination statements" (1) to point out when a boss is being over-the-top transactional and (2) to highlight the positive effects of connecting to people on a more personal level.

1. *Most of us on the team are used to your all-business approach to getting things done, but we've got some new team members who are accustomed to something very different, and they're starting to feel that things are way too impersonal here.*
2. *But there are times when you can shift into a different gear – like when you stayed around after the team dinner last week. That meant a lot to everyone – but especially to the new people who felt like it gave them a chance to relate to you in a more personal way.*

The seven qualities of social intelligence include empathy and attunement, as indicated above. The other five qualities – organizational awareness, influence, developing others, inspiration, and teamwork – provide further guidance for helping a *Perilous* boss merge EQ and SQ to be more effective.

Exercise

Clues for Helping a *Perilous* Boss
—————— Combine EQ and SQ ——————

Organizational Awareness – Making certain the boss is made aware of issues swirling around in the organization that have implications for his/her effective leadership. These issues may even involve his/her leadership style.

Influence – Your boss may not be as persuasive and influential as he/she thinks; finding ways to hold up that mirror will be key in his/her making necessary adjustments on strategy, operations, people, or whatever the issues at hand may be.

Developing Others – If your boss has neglected this, take the opportunity to raise the conversation to a more proactive level. Your behind-the-scenes and collaborative conversations with astute HR professionals both inside and outside your company should prove useful, i.e., give you more ammo to help your boss raise his/her game on this pressing issue.

Inspiration – Hope is perhaps the greatest nonmonetary currency available to any leader. Unlike *Remarkable* leaders, the *Perilous* are not as reflexively gifted or consistent at eliciting hope throughout their organizations. Unconsciously, they can be too burdened by their own "stuff" to be inspirational for others. Also, their more natural critical and judgmental behavior is not especially inspiring for most.

One way direct reports can be helpful in this regard is by giving their bosses a steady input of success stories from the trenches that they (the bosses) can use to reinforce optimistic expectations regarding the future. If they are disinclined to do this, direct reports can assume an ambassadorial role, i.e., take it upon themselves to spread balancing positive information throughout the organization.

Teamwork – In addition to aiding bosses on the assemblage/maintenance of an "A" team, subordinates can assist *Perilous* bosses immeasurably by the simple act of encouraging regular team-based interaction. Many teams that don't experience this become inured to its absence and as a result miss opportunities to grow through interdisciplinary discussions/planning, collaborating on challenging assignments, increasing the depth of collegial learning, debriefing mistakes, and the elation of celebrating mutual successes.

Example of How a *Perilous* Leader Really Blew It – A Case of Seriously Flawed EQ and SQ

A t about 10:15 am on September 11, 2001, I received a phone call from the Corporate Head of Human Resources in a global consumer brands company based in Manhattan. He explained that the most senior executive on site that horrific day was the COO who had become infuriated by people's distress and distraction from their work. He had been overheard saying to his Administrative Assistant as he slammed his office door, "This is a business not a social work agency!"

The HR head wanted my opinion about what to do. I urged him to confront the COO and to urge him to close the building ASAP so distraught employees could get home and/or continue to seek information about loved ones who were working in the World Trade Center buildings.

The building was eventually closed around 11:30 am. However, by that time, news of the COO's behavior had spread through the company like proverbial wildfire. This behavior can be viewed not only as his extreme lack of EQ and SQ but as an indication of the true content of his character and inability to lead effectively in a crisis.

Behavior Observations of *Perilous* Leaders: Three Clues for Helping Minimize their Sense of "Unrequited Work"

Perilous leaders have the potential to distinguish themselves on the three noteworthy behaviors cited in Chap. 6 as a guide for managing *Remarkable* leaders. However, these essential leadership behaviors – boldness, enterprise-wide thinking, and empowerment – can be blocked, thwarted, or otherwise delimited given the underlying sense of unrequited work among *Perilous* leaders. They may possess these behaviors but they are simply unable to use them consistently well, given behavioral habits related to caution, self-absorption, and/or a need to control.

Boldness

Behaving boldly can involve the full spectrum of business issues, including strategy, strategy execution, organization processes and policies, culture behavior norms, people management, relationship power dynamics, budgets, driving results, marketing plans, the competition, and customer relations. Since only those direct reports who have the trust and confidence of *Perilous* bosses will have the opportunity to "manage" them prior to the initiation of bold moves, a necessary precondition is to have established enough of a rapport to influence them.

With the assumption that this precondition is in place, *two compelling questions can guide effective management of a Perilous boss when it comes to his/her acting boldly*:

#1 When the bold initiative looks potentially successful, you can probe the following:

Can the boss make a convincing case for it based on patterns, facts, data, or whatever else may be needed to explain his/her action OR is it based on his/her intuition alone?

Note: If it is intuition alone, this does not necessarily scuttle the bold action, but conversation with him/her about the "intuitive leap" can help inform other conversations the boss may need to have with those senior to him/her.

#2 When the bold initiative looks ill-conceived or likely to arouse too much resistance or is ill-timed given other things going on in the organization at the time, you can probe the following:

Can the boss put-on-the-brakes at least long enough to consider how much political capital he/she can afford to burn if the bold move is made immediately?

Note: The boss may ultimately take the bold action – but that will not be without the benefit of your attempt to prompt a close reexamination of it in terms of potential success, right timing, and other "political" considerations.

Enterprise-Wide Thinking

Given their innate and business acumen capabilities, *Perilous* leaders have the potential to influence important developments with enterprise-wide effects. However, they do not always realize this potential because, once again, their state of unrequited work can get in the way. The fullness of their enterprise-wide thinking can be diminished by any number of disruptive feelings, including envy of their own bosses, competitive instincts toward peers, overall lack of trust in others, labile moods, and an intensely judgmental outlook that can derail ideas before they even get started.

It's also important to note that *Perilous* leaders compare favorably to *Remarkable* leaders in the quality of their enterprise-wide thoughts and analyses but can lack the passionate spark needed to achieve the rapid alignment and committed efforts of others. In short, their potential enterprise-wide initiatives never get the traction they deserve.

The following questions can help guide direct reports who want to influence/better manage a *Perilous* boss in terms of enterprise-wide thinking:

- What are the three top company-wide issues interfering with the organization being as successful as it could be?
- What are your specific thoughts about how to address them?
- How can I – or the team – assist you in creating a plan to resolve at least one of these issues this year?

Empowerment

Perilous leaders can really struggle with the managerial ideal of creating high-performing, empowered teams. A long list of behaviors can prevent this from happening. The three most prevalent of these behaviors are (1) arrogance (*No one knows as much as I know*), (2) micromanagement (*No one can do it as well or as fast as I can*), and (3) mistrust (*I can't trust anyone else completely – it will get screwed up unless I handle it*).

Added to arrogance, micromanagement, and mistrust is the emotional residue of their feelings of unrequited work. As related to empowerment, these feelings foster behaviors that are experienced by team members as *Perilous* leaders' chronic disappointment, frustration, cynicism, and negativity – feelings that sabotage the likelihood of fostering empowered teamwork. Instead of empowerment, team members can feel infantilized, demoralized, and unfairly criticized. Over time, the most talented among them become retention risks and often leave for other employment.

Here are a few guiding questions for direct reports who have the opportunity for and who feel courageous enough to attempt influencing a *Perilous* boss about empowerment:

- We see that you are in a constant state of overload – what specific tasks can anyone of us or the team take on to lighten your load?
- Assuming we handle these tasks well, what larger objectives would you be willing to delegate – with the proviso that you'd be receiving frequent status updates all the way through?
- What specific things do you want to see from the team that will increase your trust in our potential to deliver great results?

To summarize, the efforts direct reports make to manage the bold, enterprise-wide thinking and empowering behaviors of their *Perilous* bosses are less about the specific questions offered here and more about the *intention* to try to manage these essential leadership behaviors. These questions are provided as kindling wood for direct reports who want to light this fire – this fire of potential behavioral improvement for their bosses. These efforts may or may not be rewarded by the appreciative acceptance of *Perilous* bosses. However, if they have been preceded by other efforts that have laid the foundation for constructive, caring boss management efforts, the results can be inestimably rewarding for direct reports, as well as for their grateful bosses.

LESSON PLAN for Managing
a *Perilous* Boss

STRIVE to REDUCE BOSS'S SENSE of "UNREQUITED WORK"
Increase your concerted efforts to recognize – and affirm – their real talents and accomplishments. Replace their chronic discontent with reminders of important contributions to the organization.

ORCHESTRATE TEAM-BASED DISCUSSIONS of STRATEGY and OTHER KEY BUSINESS ISSUES
Try to increase collective thinking and brainstorming with boss; minimize boss's feelings of lonely isolation. Maximize collaboration, transparency, and trust.

USE PERSPECTIVE-MAKING TO MANAGE REAL AND/OR IMAGINED FEARS
Help your boss get the right people in the right roles, and ensure that the right conditions are created for others to succeed. Make certain hiring (as well as promotion decisions) focus equally on candidates' skills, experiences, and "fit" with the organization.

CLOTHE THE EMPEROR/EMPRESS
Keep the boss tuned into employees' real issues and concerns – including any related to the boss's leadership style.

CONNECT HEAD and HEART
Coach the boss away from behavior that is overly content-based and toward behavior that is a blend of objective and subjective factors. Give focused feedback about their (1) communication effectiveness with large and small groups, (2) behavioral consistency (mouth and feet in synch), and (3) courageous acts on behalf of the employees as well as on larger strategy or other business considerations.

INFLUENCE EMOTIONALLY INTELLIGENT BEHAVIOR
Provide observations that could help increase the boss's (1) understanding of his/her impact on others, (2) effective use of emotions, (3) attunement to and empathy for others, and (4) forming relationships that are at least somewhat personal versus just transactional.

BE A MIRROR for BOLD ACTIONS
Strive to be a helpful and trusted litmus test or set of brakes a boss can seek out and/or otherwise rely on before taking bold action.

HELP RELEASE ENTERPRISE-WIDE THINKING POTENTIAL
Be alert for ways to excite the boss's enterprise-wide thinking, decrease undue political concerns, and help propel initiatives that flourish toward value-added conclusions.

FOSTER EMPOWERED, TEAM-BASED LEADERSHIP
Be a catalyst within the team for identifying and delivering specific results that may surprise, delight, and encourage the boss's willingness to empower the team further.

End Notes

1. It is important to note that not every *Perilous* leader can receive/accept the efforts others make to "manage" them. Many are too proud or arrogant to do so; however, among these, there may be some who will eventually unfreeze enough to be helped. There are others for whom any efforts to assist their being more effective will be experienced as intrusive and/or unnecessary and will, therefore, be rejected.
2. The phrase "psychological paychecks" refers to the verbal (nonmonetary) recognition and praise of employees' successful efforts.
3. This is not to suggest that there aren't times when the use of negative emotions is a good – and necessary – thing for leaders to do. For example, when employees have really not expended their best efforts despite the boss's consistent and supportive direction, this can be a time for stern and direct admonishment and expression of disappointment.

Managing a *Toxic* Boss

*In organizations, real power and energy are generated through relationships.
The patterns of relationships and the capacities to form them are more
important than tasks, functions, roles, and positions.*

Margaret "Meg" Wheatly
Leadership and the New Science

In simplest terms, *Behind the Executive Door* is about the primacy of relationships in the workplace – especially the significant relationships between bosses and their subordinates. Thus far, we have examined how *Remarkable* bosses are likely to foster positive and growth-promoting relationships with their subordinates. We have considered the unrequited work issue that impedes *Perilous* leaders from being fully effective and forming developmentally oriented relationships. And we are alerted to the serious behavioral problems that can make working for a *Toxic* boss especially difficult.

Despite the discussion of *Toxic* leaders both in this book and in other writing (Wasylyshyn 2011a), some may doubt the prevalence of this type of leader in senior executive roles. While I no longer coach them, they are out there.[1] They are out there because many of them are smart, sly, and can deliver results, and as long as the results are there, their bosses leave them in place. The question is *at what cost to others* do they deliver their results? Even the most cursory trip down business's memory lane reveals a rogues' gallery of business leaders who delivered results but were later indicted, sent to prison, or were otherwise shamed from their positions of power given behavior that can be described as psychopathic. Ronson (2011) wrote of former Sunbeam CEO, Al Dunlap, "FAST COMPANY included him in an article about potentially psychopathic CEOs... referring to his poor behavioral controls and his lack of empathy.

We have witnessed the financial greed of leaders to include Kenneth Lay (Enron), Jeffrey Skilling (Enron), Dennis Kozlowski (Tyco), Bernie Ebbers (WorldCom), and Chung Mong Koo (Hyundai). Sexual harassers and/or marital cheaters include Mark Hurd (HP), Charles Phillips (Oracle), Harry Stonecipher (Boeing), and Dov Charney, CEO of American Apparel. In addition to being sued many times for sexual harassment, Charney had had numerous affairs with female subordinates and was known to walk around his office in his underwear.

The large number of political power figures pulled down by their zippers include Gary Hart, Barney Frank, Bill Clinton, John Edwards, Rudy Giuliani, Newt Gingrich, Jim McGreevey, Mark Sanford, and Eliot Spitzer. But this is America, and these men have either resuscitated their careers or may have the opportunity to do so. Why this is so – even in an era of such behavior scrutiny – is a topic for another time. Back to managing *Toxic* bosses …

—— Example – Trying to Coach a *Toxic* Boss ——

James was raided from another consumer products company to head the failing division of a global conglomerate. While he was judged to be a brilliant strategic thinker with strong marketing instincts, he had "bad chemistry" with his direct reports almost immediately. He assessed them as "worthless and lazy" and regularly lambasted them in staff meetings – whenever he held such meetings, which was rare because he usually stayed behind the closed door to his office.

In the first 4 months of his employment, three Administrative Assistants resigned due to his "uncivil" and "overly demanding" behavior. When his Human Resources partner tried to speak to him about the growing discontentment among his entire staff, James scoffed saying, "I'm on a turnaround mission here and if they can't take the heat, I'm throwing them all out of the kitchen."

Eventually, a coach was brought in to gather 360 data, give James feedback, and help him adjust his behavior so the company could benefit from what he had to offer. James resented the intervention, was barely civil to the coach, blew up when he received the feedback, and threatened to "… sue everyone on the landscape for slander." Ultimately, his boss carefully tracked James's results and he was eventually fired for missing most of his annual objectives.

The serious limitations of *Toxic* bosses both psychologically and within the context of the leadership competencies, EQ/SQ, and behaviors as discussed in previous chapters, necessitate a different approach regarding potential ways to "manage" them. Actually, the guidance offered in this chapter is more about how to "survive" a *Toxic* boss.

This approach is guided by a core question: *Can I continue to work for this Toxic boss?* There are always financial and other practical reasons that affect one's willingness to even consider this question. But in the interest of your overall well-being – physically, mentally, emotionally, professionally, and personally – I believe you must ask yourself this question. And whatever your answer to this question might be, the rest of this chapter is focused on ways to help you survive well with that answer.

First, let's get some data. The following STAY-GO exercise has been designed to help you assess carefully whether you can continue working for your *Toxic* boss or not. You may think you are as decided as you need to be, or you may realize you need greater clarity. Wherever you are on this continuum of *knowing whether or not you can work for your Toxic boss*, the following exercise should be helpful. In other words, it will provide you a methodical way to assess whether you want to STAY or GO.

Exercise

Working for a *Toxic* Boss: Should I Stay ——————— or Should I Go? ———————

Exercise instruction:

1. To make this exercise as relevant as possible to your current situation:
   - Read all the factors.
   - IGNORE factors that do not apply.
   - Add new factors under the "Other" section – factors that match you current situation.
   - Make a copy of this exercise *before* you fill it out. You may want to have someone who knows you well fill it out independent of you. Comparing your respective ratings should prove useful.
2. Rate each factor on a 1 to 5 scale, with 5 as the highest rating. For each relevant factor, place a rating in *both* the *STAY* and *GO* columns.
   - For example, if you think the *Relationship with Boss* factor is very negative, you would put a 1 or 2 under *STAY* and a 4 or 5 under *GO*.
   - Conversely, if you think the *Opportunity to Learn* factor is quite positive, you would put a 4 or 5 under *STAY* and a 1 or 2 under *GO*.
3. Add the scores you've placed in both columns. A big difference (more than ten points) in the *STAY–GO* ratings is a clear signal in favor of the *STAY* or *GO* option, i.e., the column with the highest score.
4. If there is not a big difference in the *STAY–GO* ratings, this indicates a caution for you to reflect carefully and make sure you do not make an impetuous decision.
5. If you are inclined to join another organization, have multiple meetings with and get as much information as you can about a prospective new boss. In other words, you want to avoid going from one *Toxic* boss to another!

Rate factors on a 1–5 scale, 5 being highest.

Factors	STAY	GO
A desire to pursue something different altogether (e.g., MBA, law school, other grad school study)		
Autonomy – level of empowerment		
Creative latitude – freedom to pursue/apply one's own ideas		
Daily level of stress		
Free time – implications of work demands for work-personal integration		
Fun – work has its lighter moments, too		
Intellectual stimulation		
Job security		
Money (current)		
Money (future potential)		
Negative effects of this role on my personal life (stress)		
Pace of work – fast, medium, slow. Consistent with one's preference?		
Peerage – relationships with peers strong enough to tolerate adverse effects of boss behavior		
Potential for *Toxic* boss being removed from role		
Potential for me to get another role in the organization (not reporting to this *Toxic* boss)		
Power – ability to influence boss and others		
Professional legacy – work provides opportunity to mentor, teach, influence others		
Recognition – stature, respect for work done		
Relationships (colleagues, staff)		
Relationships (personal) – likelihood of forming work-based friendships		
Relationship with boss – effects of this in terms of mood, morale, motivation		
Resources – staff and other resources needed to meet job objectives		
Span of impact – opportunity to influence others in the organization		
Travel – enough opportunity to travel; travel is not excessive		
Visibility to senior management		
Work environment/location – comfort, positive esthetics; reasonable commute		
Other factors (if any)		
Other factors (if any)		
Other factors (if any)		
Totals		

Now that you have "tested" and perhaps answered with a greater degree of clarity whether or not you can continue to work for your *Toxic* boss, the effort of trying to "survive" him/her can begin. Or perhaps it is not a beginning – perhaps it is a resumption of an effort that didn't yield enough before. If so, may your efforts be reinvigorated by the certainty of what you need to do now, i.e., STAY or start an effort to GO.

Two Major Lessons for Surviving a *Toxic* Boss (1) Peerage and (2) Planning an Escape

Lesson #1: Peerage

What is intended by the term "peerage" is the close bond that can be formed among people working in the same organization and more specifically for the same *Toxic* boss. This type of bonding involves the intentional effort of employees to better deal with their shared misfortune of having a *Toxic* boss. There are four interrelated aspects of peerage (1) communication, (2) unity, (3) internal locus of control, and (4) problem-solving. See Fig. 8.1.

─────────────── **A *Toxic* Boss** ───────────────

This brilliant founder and CEO of a national consulting firm had been in a religious order for many years before he entered the business world. As one of his partners said, "If you want to understand Grant, just think God complex." While few knew much about Grant's early years, there were stories about an emotionally deprived childhood, physical beatings for discipline, and his deep-seated bitterness that influenced the domination and hostile aspects of his leadership. However, his stunning conceptual thinking ability coupled with shrewd marketing instincts and charismatic speaking skill enabled him to launch a company that distinguished itself quickly especially given the talented first group of partners he recruited to the enterprise.

While Grant could "seduce" talented people to the firm, he had difficulty retaining them. Most had the same experience of being "abandoned" by him quickly and receiving little affirmation for their committed and successful efforts. The pattern of his moodiness, cutting remarks, negative body language, hostility, and bad-mouthing others behind their backs spread over the firm like sleet. Administrative staff members often hid in the restrooms during his infamous tirades. The consultants united, i.e., bonded together to minimize the damaging effects of Grant's outbursts and to identify specific solutions that would help ease/solve recurring issues.

Grant could excite the consulting staff with the quality of his ideas, but he failed at leading them given the intensity of his self-absorption and inherent meanness. With a reputation for "going after" people who disappointed him, he once traveled in an ambulance with a manager who had taken ill at the office – berating the manager the entire way to the hospital about his poor quarterly results.

The firm would witness a revolving door of consultants – but none ever as fully capable as the group Grant had first recruited to the firm. All of these left to create their own ventures or to join competing companies. Grant's firm continued for several years but he failed to invest adequately in the next product wave and was stuck in a business space rapidly commoditizing. Fortuitously, his timing for selling the firm was just right; he did so at a significant profit but he died soon thereafter.

Communication

The reactions of people reporting to a *Toxic* boss vary widely. Many can suffer in silence, simmer in anger, be combative, or become inured to even the worst aspects of the leader's behavior. Some may display a business version of "Stockholm Syndrome."[2] The key point here is that people with *Toxic* bosses need to reach out and talk to each other about their respective and/or collective experiences. It is through steady communication with each other that they can keep a firm grip on reality and not suffer in silence.

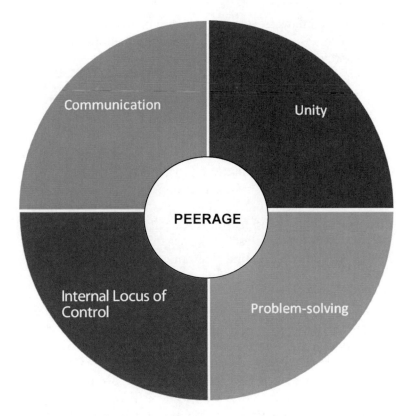

Fig. 8.1 Lesson #1 For surviving a *Toxic* boss

Example of Using Communication to Lessen the Sting of *Toxic* Bosses

For over 20 years, the R&D division of a global company was run by a succession of super-critical alpha males epitomized by one who installed an infrared lighting system on his desert vehicle so he could watch tarantulas mate at night. The sum effect of these *Toxic* leaders was a culture where aggressive attacking and hostile "gotchas" ruled. As one scientist said, "It's one thing to have to defend my science, I've been trained to do that. It's another thing to have to deal with this constant sniping and to fight for respect day in and day out."

While the time employees working in this company spent communicating about the problems with various *Toxic* bosses was helpful for them, untold hours of productivity were lost to the corporation.

Unity

Toxic leaders, like Grant in the sidebar example, often try to divide and conquer in their efforts to dominate and to get their needs met. Since these needs are not always congruent with pressing business priorities, it is wise for direct reports to stay united on their views as related to these urgent issues. The best way to stand firm in these efforts of unity is to position them as being in the best interests of the organization and to have the facts and data to back that up. Over time, incremental successes with this "enterprise defense" may be seen and appreciated by some *Toxic* leaders for what it is at its core: an effort to save them from themselves.

When subordinates' best unification efforts are turned away (*There's no way I can consider what you're suggesting*) or sabotaged by the leader (*I know you're not really questioning my leadership or suggesting that I take that dumb action, are you?*), they may have to take their united efforts to the next level, i.e., the boss's boss. Whenever this step is taken, it must be supported with many specific examples of the *Toxic* leader's flawed leadership and how it is adversely affecting the productivity and morale of the team, business unit, department, or whatever the case may be.

Internal Locus of Control

The intensity, unpredictability, and piercing nature of a *Toxic* leader's attacks and tirades can knock even psychologically sturdy and resilient people off stride. One astute Human Resources (HR) Director who had been working for such a boss for a year said, "It's like slipping on banana peels daily – even though you can see the big yellow flashing danger on the road, you can't avoid it, and you know you're going to fall on your ass whether you deserve to or not. The key thing to remember is that 95% of the time, it's *not* about you."

The key words in this HR Director's comment were, "…95% of the time it's *not* about you." Subordinates who personalize, i.e., take personally, the often harsh and unfair comments of a *Toxic* boss are likely to suffer in the reporting relationship more than is healthy or wise. A potentially powerful antidote or tool against such personalizing is a principle from social psychology – internal locus of control. People with high internal locus of control believe that they can control their lives based on confidence in their personal assets to include the way they think and experience events. In other words, they are not at the mercy of powerful others such as the *Toxic* boss, fate, or chance. People with internal locus of control assume their efforts will be successful, can control their behavior, can be appropriately "political" if need be, and can usually influence others effectively.

Example of Using Internal Locus of Control to Deal with a *Toxic* Boss

S enior members of the top sales team in a regional consulting firm had grown weary of the outbursts of their boss at the weekly sales review meeting, and they could see the toll these "unjustified rants" were taking on talented new members of the team. After a particularly contentious meeting, a number of them assembled without the boss and decided to reinforce among each other and with the younger team members too the mantra, "It's not about me." This proved quite helpful.

Months later when they wore their "It's not about me" tee shirts to the firm's annual softball game, the self-deluded boss thought it indicated their team spirit.

Problem-Solving

When groups of people and/or team members communicate, unify, and maintain internal locus of control, the potential for proactive problem-solving is magnified. Specifically, enough energy, planning, and courage can be channeled toward finding ways to survive the *Toxic* boss. This is in contrast to just being worn down or capitulating to the demands and unjustified or insulting treatment of the boss. While there are situations when active problem-solving may be blocked completely by the resistance and power of the *Toxic* boss, there are other times when at least palliative effects can be achieved.

In the example of Grant provided above, a few of his top consultants suggested that the firm could benefit from some of its own medicine, specifically an organization survey. In his private briefing of the results with

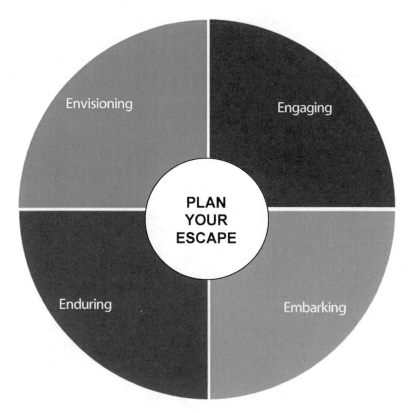

Fig. 8.2 Lesson #2 For surviving a *Toxic* boss

the external consultant, Grant was displeased about the negative view of his leadership and insisted this information not be shared with the senior team. However, there was enough other helpful data that at least neutralized some of the adverse things that were going on in the firm.

Lesson #2: Planning An Escape

If based on the STAY–GO exercise at the outset of this chapter you have decided you can no longer work for your *Toxic* boss, then it is time to *plan your escape*. Keep in mind that this may take some time; however, also know that your having made this decision should trigger the positive psychological effects of seeing light at the end of the proverbial tunnel. There are four key elements in planning an escape well (1) envisioning, (2) engaging, (3) enduring, and (4) embarking. See Fig. 8.2.

Envisioning

The first – and critical – step in planning a great escape is to *envision* a path forward. You may not know all the steps toward getting on this path, and you may not even be able to see specific signposts along the path. However *directionally* you see your way out of where you are, you have at least some idea(s) of what you would like to do next, and surely you know the kind of environment you want to work in so you can thrive personally and make a contribution. You may even be thinking of leveraging your experience and knowledge by going entrepreneurial. The point here *is giving yourself permission to envision your next path*. Then you can begin to explore how you can make it happen – this is where you will need to engage others.

Engaging

The second step in planning a great escape is to *engage* others whom you know and trust in discussions of your future. You will urge them to be frank and to *engage* so you get their constructive feedback. Through this constructive feedback, you will be able to further shape your thoughts about the path out from where you are now. It is important to note that as tempting as it may be, you will not just be *running out* of where you are. Rather, you will be *running toward* an exit you have planned carefully.

Another round of conversation would be with people who are actually doing what you have identified as a viable next direction for yourself. You want to probe key questions with them to include: *How did they get to do what they're doing? What do they like about it? What don't they like about it? What's the upside potential? What's the downside?*

If you are really not certain what you would like to do next, then you would be wise to seek help from a career management specialist. This type of professional will be able to maintain objectivity as he/she studies your background, motivated abilities, specific skills, and aspirations. After a careful analysis, this person can guide you toward career directions that make sense. A list of seasoned career management specialists is provided in Appendix F.

Enduring

The contemplation of any personal change like a career move/job change will bring both positive feelings of excitement/anticipation (*This is going to be great for me*) and anxiety (*OMG, what am I doing? How am I going to get this done? Is this going to work out for me?*).

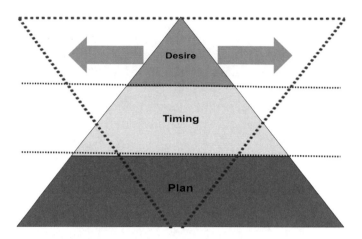

NOTE: While having a *plan* and the *timing* being right are important elements in making a personal change, the **desire** to make the change is what sustains a concerted effort, helps one manage anxiety, and calms sleepless nights.

Fig. 8.3 Key elements in making a personal change

It's important that you anticipate this see-sawing of emotion, i.e., that you *endure* it – as a normal part of the change. You will also be helped by spending time with people who "get" what you want to do and are encouraging of and upbeat about your pursuing your objective. Finally, remember that when you wake up in the middle of the night in a sweat about what you're doing or are contemplating doing, it's not the plan or even the timing of it that'll get you through and help you sustain your effort. It's the intensity of your *desire* for the goal that will keep you steady and focused. See Fig. 8.3.

I'll use myself as an example. After nearly 10 years in a career as a trade journalist at McGraw-Hill, a global publishing company, I faced the fact that I was getting nowhere fast. While my boss wasn't *Toxic*, he provided no help or encouragement in terms of career progress. Even worse, he kept asking me, *When are you going to start having children?* A fortuitous meeting with someone in the behavioral sciences and his encouragement that I should consider graduate school and a career in psychology helped me see a new path forward. Once I was accepted into graduate school, there were many sleepless nights when I wondered, *How am I going to get through this*?! The one thing that helped me endure this anxiety was the intensity of my desire to make a break with one career and turn toward another that I believed was a better fit for me. And the rest as they say, is history.

Embarking

Now is the time for *embarking* – to create a plan for your great escape – assuming you have completed some combination of the following steps (1) decided to leave where you are, (2) tested your idea for your change with others – including those who are doing what you're interested in doing, (3) have received the assistance of a career management professional, and (4) have an unshakeable desire to pursue what you've identified as your next career chapter.

Ideally, your plan is a sequential listing of specific actions and a realistic timeline for completion of each action. This plan is another aspect of a career transition with which you can receive assistance from a career management advisor. Once your plan for embarking on your future is in place, then it's all about *working the plan*. As a very wise career management consultant once told me, "The process of identifying your next job or career move should become your job until you get to where you want to be." Where you *need to be* may be a similar job to the one you have now, it may be a shift toward something else, it might be graduate school – whatever it is, it is NOT where you are now, and knowing that your time with this *Toxic* boss is time-limited should make your remaining time there more palatable.

Strive to never burn a bridge – even when leaving a *Toxic* boss. When you are ready to exit, be certain to (1) provide plenty of notice (a month, if possible), (2) suggest a successor (if there is one) or an alternate way your responsibilities can be handled, (3) resist full disclosure (except to your closest colleagues) of how your *Toxic* boss was catalytic in the decision to leave, and (4) (gulp) thank your boss for whatever it is for which you are grateful. Given the speed with which information travels, you want to stay on the high road, and this can have unanticipated benefits later, for example, when/if you ever need a reference for a new employer.

Finally, if your plan is to become employed elsewhere, try to sequence your start so that you have sufficient time for rest and resuscitation before you begin your next job. You may not realize it, but it will be beneficial to put your *Toxic* boss experience completely behind you. Specifically, you want to avoid having any psychological residue from a bad work experience contaminating your excitement and openness to a new situation. Also, if there is not an assimilation process used at your new employer, identify someone who's been there for awhile – someone you connect well to right away and who can serve as a "culture guide" as you settle in and find your ways to have impact there. You especially want to learn all you can about how to connect to and work well with your new boss. Remember, if you have chosen well, this boss should be mostly *Remarkable* – and you will be focused on establishing a reciprocal working rhythm with him/her.

Planning an Escape Can Soothe the "Insanity"

Daniel once said he wasn't sure if he was a classic "late bloomer" or just a "goof-off who lucked out." The people who reported to him during his years as a senior executive in a global manufacturing company would choose other words to describe him. These words included "jerk," "idiot," and "loser." While he was eventually fired, no one quite understood why he lasted as long as he did. Most believed it was because he had a longstanding relationship with the CEO who recruited him to the company and gave him more air cover than his performance ever warranted.

A heavy drinker and philanderer, female employees found his non-verbal behavior toward them repulsive. A few complained that instances of his behavior at off-site meetings were dangerously close to sexual harassment. His direct reports complained of his erratic management and chaos-making. Over the years, many were especially bitter about his failure to give them accurate assessments of their performance, as well as of his inattention to their ongoing development. Many talented people sought other roles in the organization. In the words of one of his Directors, "Being able to see your way out is the main way you cope with the insanity while you're still here."

The most egregious example of his bad leadership judgment – of what he called "team building" – involved a trip made to a farm that raised wild boars. Team members were given knives and the instruction to chase a group of greased pigs, catch one, and slit its throat until it was dead. (For the metaphorical rendition of this event, see "Killing Pigs" in Chap. 9.)

Daniel's intention was to provide a "memorable" team-building experience for his all-male team – an experience that would "surpass anything" they had ever done before. This florid example of Toxic leadership fueled by Daniel's narcissism and negligible understanding of how to motivate a team raises a serious question about his suitability for any leadership responsibility at all.

LESSON PLAN for Surviving
—————————— a *TOXIC BOSS* ——————————

- Use the Stay–Go Exercise in this chapter to inform your decision.
- IF YOU DECIDED TO STAY, LEVERAGE PEERAGE – ESTABLISH/ DEEPEN PEER RELATIONSHIPS AT WORK. STAY FOCUSED ON:
- Fostering frequent and open communication with peers about boss-related behavior as an antidote to over-personalizing troubling events.
- Uniting with peers on key issues especially when the boss is more self-focused than on what's in the best interests of the business.
- Maintaining strong internal locus of control, i.e., the belief that you can control your work-related destiny given your talents, experiences, commitment to the organization, and purity of intention about the work that needs to get accomplished.
- Bonding with peers for proactive problem-solving on issues that need to be resolved for the enterprise to be successful.

IF YOU DECIDE TO GO, PLAN YOUR ESCAPE. STAY FOCUSED ON:

- Envisioning a viable future elsewhere.
- Engaging others who know you well in serious and comprehensive conversation about the options you are considering.
- Enduring the inevitable anxiety that can arise when one contemplates a change in work; strive to balance such anxiety with the strong desire for your "next thing" – even if it may take some time to achieve.
- Embarking upon the future with a well-thought-out plan and guidance from the resources you need to ensure that your plan is viable and makes sense for who you are and where you are in life currently.
- If you are joining another company, be certain to assess the likelihood of a good "fit" between your new boss and you.

IF YOU GET INTO ESCAPE MODE, STAY ON THE HIGH ROAD WHEN YOU TELL YOUR *TOXIC* BOSS AND OTHERS IN THE COMPANY THAT YOU ARE LEAVING. REMEMBER:

- You may need a reference from this boss some day.
- There were probably some things you gained during this employment, and it would be wise for you to acknowledge this as you leave.
- The reality of others who, for their own reasons, must continue working for the *Toxic* boss. Be attuned to and have empathy for their concerns versus displaying too much zeal about your good fortune.

- To maintain contact with your best peers, direct reports, and others – networks have never been as critical as they are now.
- The importance of having a break between leaving your *Toxic* boss and your next pursuit – whatever it may be. You need time to rest, readjust, heal, and clear your head to be fully ready for your next work challenge.
- If there is not an assimilation process in your next company, ask for a "culture guide" to help ensure that you settle in well.
- Learn everything you can about your new boss – and forge as much of a reciprocal working relationship with him/her as possible.

End Notes

[1] I have serious reservations about the coachability of *Toxic* leaders because too much ego or psychological dysfunction gets in the way of their willingness to open up and learn. Further, for many, the prospect of change represents something they must defend against. In short, trying to coach a *Toxic* leader can be a serious waste of time for all involved, raise expectations that cannot be delivered on, and be a bad financial investment because the ROI is simply not going to be there.

[2] "Stockholm Syndrome" is a paradoxical psychological phenomenon wherein people held hostage can express adulation and have positive feelings toward their captors. This was offered as an interpretation of what happened to Patty Hearst when she was abducted by the Symbionese Liberation Army (SLA) in the 1970s. There can be a psychological corollary for long-term employees reporting to *Toxic* bosses, i.e., this is a way to understand why they remain – especially when they are in comfortable working conditions and feel well-cared for financially.

The Power of Metaphor: A Tool for Further Reflection on Leadership Behavior

The American poet Ulys H. Yates said, "The poet makes the specific universal" (Wasylyshyn 2011a, p. 12). My specific observations of business leaders – these *Remarkable*, *Perilous*, and *Toxic* types – are representative of executive behavior as I have witnessed it. My intention is to make these types universally understood and useful to a broader audience. I believe the understanding of these types has important implications for the effectiveness of business leaders, for the development of people who report to them, and ultimately, for the success of their organizations.

Several years ago, after having identified these three leadership types, I considered various ways to convey these observations to the general public. Initially, I planned to write a book of comprehensive case studies. However, I felt more challenged to find a way to convey this information that was less full of my "data," interpretations, descriptions or recommendations about executive effectiveness. I looked for a way that would peak interest and prompt insights but would not lead readers anywhere – not anywhere other than into their own thoughts and free associations about leaders.

Going back to Yates, I settled on the power of metaphor. More specifically, I wrote a series of poems or *executive vignettes* as I sometimes refer to them. In the spare lines of these vignettes, I pierced to core aspects of leadership behavior but left the interpretation of each vignette to the reader. While each vignette is accompanied by explanatory material, readers are invited to linger in the white space around the poems – to linger here long enough for their own thoughts about leaders to emerge. Lingering here may evoke unspoken truths about and possibilities for leaders. In this sense, the power of metaphorical thought can catalyze the potential of subordinates being more than cautious mirrors. They can manage their bosses by becoming weavers – informed and courageous weavers of the truth their bosses need to have to be fully effective.

K.M. Wasylyshyn, *Behind the Executive Door: Unexpected Lessons for Managing Your Boss and Career*, DOI 10.1007/978-1-4614-0376-0_9,
© Karol M. Wasylyshyn 2012

In other words, the catalytic moment or set of experiences that influenced the writing of each poem matter infinitely less than what is evoked for the reader. Think of these evocations as a source of energy to sweep any psychological debris off the boss-subordinate landscape. On *this* cleared, uncluttered landscape much is possible including enough separation from the self to "see" the more powerful other (in organization hierarchy terms) including *their* struggles with inner demons, bosses, and the people who report to them. In this sense, the potential for empathic resonance with a boss is increased exponentially and what emerges is a heightened reciprocity – or the glue for what can become a true working partnership.

While particular executives have provided catalytic sparks for these poems, it's important to note that they are based on common themes in the lives business leaders. In this sense, each poem is a condensation of many executives who represent a theme – and leader type. The poems in this chapter involve themes that include executives dealing with uncertainty, giving motivational feedback, resisting candid feedback, making bad hiring decisions, managing employees humanistically, wielding unbridled power, and navigating critical life phase transitions.

Further, the verse and images in this chapter can evoke memories of a stellar *Remarkable* boss, a chronically discontented *Perilous* boss, or an irrational and abusive *Toxic* one. They may trigger an awareness of how a boss relationship could have been handled differently. They may prompt a quiet contemplation of how to better collaborate with and manage the boss you have now. At minimum, these illustrations of three leadership types will serve to increase one's ability to distinguish among them. Further, I hope they will serve to embed in the business mainstream the language for this behaviorally based leadership typology: *Remarkable, Perilous* and *Toxic*. This language – these names of leader types – can aid more focused and accurate decisions about leaders to include selection, promotion and succession planning.

Finally, remember, that your boss (or you) is not consistently one of these leader types. Circumstances can influence movement along the continuum of *Remarkable, Perilous*, and *Toxic* behavior – in both one's work and personal life. The challenge is to help bosses (and perhaps yourself) to be *Remarkable* most of the time.

The following four executive vignettes provide examples of *Remarkable* leaders.

THE SOLIDITY OF FOG

He would step into it early

as it tumbled low over the land

but high enough to envelop him

morning scapular

that he could embrace

press onto himself

kiss as a totem

certainty in the quiet,

clarity in the calm

as he worked the right problem

alone in this sudden place

mysterious in its habits

and the fog

the fog was the only

thing he could

trust completely.

Discussion of Vignette

Finding himself in Asia for the first time, this business leader is simultaneously in the grip of its utter unfamiliarity and its enigmatic beauty both rolling over him as a fog of uncertainty. However, his clarity and confidence transcend all uncertainty. He remains calm relying on his internal locus of control–what he knows, what he's done, his skills, his instincts, and the force of his will to achieve objectives.

MOURNING IN KYOTO

I see her gazing into the ryokan garden …
bittersweet reverie I think until she says,

"It takes a lifetime

to just sit and stare

watching a rain drop

drop

from one leaf

to another below."

Discussion of Vignette

The uncommon empathy and generosity of an emotionally attuned boss helped one of his key managers mourn the loss of her husband. Knowing that she was an avid gardener, he encouraged the inclusion of Kyoto on a business trip she took to Asia. While walking the gardens there, she began a journey back to herself – a self that still embraced her marital identity but also started to separate from it.

EMPTY NEXT

We escaped it again, didn't we?
You Freudian-slipped nest to next –
do you remember, an hour ago at lunch
that quick creeping up to
that semi-glow feel of it
that open, brave dew of it
like we were really on it?
Then the fading … fast fading away from it;
we are strong masters of elusion you and I
even knowing It is the silken thread
to open, or lift the heart anew.
If you lie still, I will pull it gently through your throat
this will not hurt,
there will be no blood
it will be a sudden sliding and
when you see it – NO, when you hold it
it will become your kite's string and
you will fly – fly mighty from your familiar nest;
empty will become full again.
Let me pull it … let me pull it …
let me pull it now, and we can soar together.

Discussion of Vignette

The conundrum of *meaning* is exacerbated for this CEO by the "empty nest" phase of life. Her younger child now gone to college, what did she really desire to do next? Her Freudian slip of the word "next" for "nest" during a luncheon with the author opened an important conversation about *legacy*. With this as an organizing principle, she was relieved of the existential *what next* question, identified a few compelling goals, and used her exquisite leadership skills to make them happen.

DUENDE

The words fall into each other rolling over and over
smooth, steady ball bouncing between them
the room drenched in an amber light
as their breathing ... their breathing keeps moving
moving in a rhythm soothing the weight of the hour
and their eyes, their eyes locked onto each other whilst
dismissing the assembled papers on the table
the papers masquerading as real information.

Neither one of them notices the fly –
big buzzing house fly that's broken through,
it careens from window to ceiling to wall unable to land
but they never see it – so intent in their words, words buzzing
buzzing back and forth intensity and unity with the fly
for they are strangers, too but their words, their words keep falling
landing into each other rolling over and over into the amber light.

Nothing will be left unsaid ... there is no perch for confusion,
no berth for resting, no corner for escaping the words
all the words are being said – and heard
... heard over and over as each provides a bench for the other.
They are stepping from moss to wet rock without slipping,
they are building a bridge to the table cleared and set anew.
They have maintained reverence for the past, shed truth on the present,
and staged the future for change: coveted vermillion gate.
This was not the usual performance review.

Discussion of Vignette

With enormous personal magnetism and charm, this C-suite executive
has eased his direct report's anxiety and turned the annual performance
review into a rare and inspirational conversation. This conversation is
anchored in an atmosphere of hope and passion about the future, a future
they will co-create. In the fading light of this important afternoon, there is
a fierceness about the power of candor and clarity. We are reminded that
the most remarkable leaders are relentlessly motivational, open, and strive
to ignite the necessary excitement and alignment among the people whom
they lead.

The following four executive vignettes are based on themes representative of *Perilous* leaders.

NIGHT MOVES

Two martinis and

a bottle of Chardonnay later,

he's as loose as rain,

as expansive as paint,

and ready to sleep for the first time

since be became CEO.

But sleep rarely came again

having been hijacked by images of

snakes, leopards, lizards, tigers,

every member of his Board –

and an especially haunting hyena

with his mother's face,

and her endless ferocity.

Discussion of Vignette

This new CEO's concerns about his effectiveness in the role, as well as his unspoken hope for parental approval, dominate *Night Moves*. Convenient target of his mother's lifelong despondency over her own unrealized career goals, he endured the brunt of her self-repulsion that spread over him like sleet.

EMPEROR'S JACKET

The thickening quiet and ice – he could not know

what lie on the new path before him or who,

hidden in the bracken, awaited his trial there.

He did not see that the emperor's silk jacket

was really knotted and spotted with mud …

it had felt so smooth and generous at the table

when they beckoned each other

into a union of lasting effects.

He had not seen the photos of prey

dripping blood from the tiger's mouth

on the wall there; blood that would soon

intermingle with his – he careening in a mire

barely half his own making.

Discussion of Vignette

In this new-hire-gone-bad situation, the *Perilous* boss (emperor) plays out a classic seduction-abandonment scenario instead of fully aiding his new manager's assimilation into the company. Adrift in a culture of alpha males, and with a boss who did not fully support the work his subordinate was hired to do, the new manager left the company after several difficult months. On deeper reflection, he recognized his role in this ill-fated circumstance given a combination of compelling factors that included his not pushing harder for specifics regarding his role, the company culture, and his boss's leadership style.

LAHORE 2006

Dust and trash intermingle with the scent of time here
dignity and grace infuse it further, seductive bouquet
as the businessmen sit on silk divans doing business
sipping tea, sidelong glances, white towels for sweat.

Sweat drips from others, too – the men pulling hay;
hard, serpentine pulling of hay around animals and merchants
tireless pulling as the hay falls on the dirt, this dirt the road
of the road more traveled – but without signpost or lane.

She takes this road to the border,
border where the soldiers strut at sunset
strutting for the people waving flags
people waving flags on both sides of the border
flags defiant in more distance than possibility.

Throngs on both sides of the border are roaring
fist-pumping, twirling and whirling for their nations
their nations where there is more dirt than truth,
more hype than stability, more plots than sanity,
and soon, more blood in the dirt near the border
the border where the strutting goes on unabated
as the businessmen keep on with their business and tea.

Discussion of Vignette

The "she" in *Lahore 2006* is a local employee of an American-owned company with an office in Pakistan. A talented manager but with ambivalent career and personal aspirations, she is both attached to and frustrated by the limitations of her homeland – limitations that, along with her ambivalence – perpetuated her state of "unrequited work." We are also reminded that commerce continues – and can thrive – even in the midst of chaos, poverty, and the potential of political calamity.

THE CORPORATE ABCs

Amazons join the gladiators now
Battle-scarred and proven
Corporate-crusted and as
Darwinian in pursuit of their results
Exceptional results
Fiercer and fiercer the stretch
Goals in a symbiotic dancing with
Habits – tribal habits
Indigenous as the
Just-in-time apologies offered to
Keep the family steady … everyone still in
Love enough even when the
Milestone events are missed
Never to be seen again because work
Obligations will usually trump the
Possibility of
Quality time with a child – or other close
Relation. Amazons need sleep but
Sleep isn't working as they are
Turning into cold backs … backs that trigger
Uneasy promises and everyone's
Very
Weary of the deepening chill
Xylophone shrill ringing through their beds as another
Year of promises adds up to
Zero.

Discussion of Vignette

While the number of female executives in top corporate roles is still below 5%, incremental gains continue. From a work-family integration perspective, the lives of these successful women parallel those of their male peers: the intensity of trying to juggle both spheres of life, and the inevitable family resentments that can accrue over time.

The following executive vignettes provide examples of four *Toxic* leaders that can be found in both privately-held and public companies.

SPIN ME

I saw the monster

sudden radioactive glint

from the corner office

terror and toxin

spreading

people walking backwards

in the tangled quiet

contamination spreading

spreading fast

to the wires

wires now stripped down

Stark

to the truth ...

truth tinder box

tinder box of truth

ignited, and he's revealed;

but he'll not tolerate

this intrusion. He

strikes another flame

his spinning top ablaze now

furious burn ... to ashes

destruction enough

to satisfy

his ravenous delusion.

Discussion of Vignette

Despite the widespread use of "executive 360 feedback" and its proven value as a leadership development tool, many executives are not open to this type of data – especially when it runs counter to their view of themselves. For psychopaths or unproductive narcissists, in particular, their glittering self images have been carefully crafted from the outset of a career – along with their reflexive defensiveness to protect these personas. Their defensive behavior can include denial, projection, withdrawal and rationalization. *Spin Me* captures an executive's instantaneous fury about – and burning need to defend against his feedback.

CRACKED

There is a crack in his head

his head has a crack

a crack full of crackers

clogging his thinking with crumbs

crumbs falling out of his head

onto the floor, over the desks

and the chairs of his company

abundance of dirt

and egg shells ... hip deep in egg shells and dirt.

They pull on their armor, navy wool gabardine

brushed clean in steel spinning booths;

they strap into the spinning booths daily

– furious turning as the brushes

clean and baste them in revision enough

for King Crumb to bind them in promises.

There is more dirt than reason,

more crackers than time,

more time than truth

most are too stuffed to move

but the others ...

the others have opted for sanity.

Discussion of Vignette

King Crumb is the flawed second-generation leader of a medium-sized family-owned business. While he has serious psychological issues, there is no one to whom he must report and no scrutiny of a Board of Directors to temper his bad leadership behavior. His employees either feel trapped in the maelstrom or have become inured to the dysfunction of it all; they carry on despite great emotional havoc and uncertainty. Promises of fantastic financial rewards keep his most talented employees for a time but eventually they leave to work in healthier organization cultures.

STRANDED

If you went to the roof of his building at night

lantern lit, swinging it once to the left and three to the right,

they would signal back – once to the left and three to the right

over and over these low stars on the sea

shooting once to the left and three to the right

these stranded workers on ice, no possibility

but to wait for his light once to the left and three to the right

ready again … for him to feed of their waning vitality.

Discussion of Vignette

Metaphorically, there are leaders who fall in and out of love with their employees. As one Vice President in a management consulting firm said of its Founder and CEO, "One day you're up with him, the next you're in Siberia." This behavior is common among executives with bipolar disorder. It is also common among insecure leaders with a bottomless need to have their egos fed – fed in myriad ways that include accolades, new business, flawless employees, perfect children, adoring spouses, material objects, and secret lovers. In *Stranded*, employees have been cast into their metaphorical Siberia – albeit knowing they will have other chances to perform when their unpredictable boss needs them again.

KILLING PIGS

He took them to a place

where they chased wild pigs,

wrestled them to the ground,

and slit their throats dead.

Blood-smeared and breathless,

now this was a team

Building.

Discussion of Vignette

This sales executive wanted to give the members of his team an uncommon and memorable developmental experience. While it was both uncommon and memorable, it was not developmental. Further, this example of bad judgment raises serious questions about someone like this holding any leadership responsibility.

About the Author

Karol M. Wasylyshyn's business career has evolved through the disciplines of journalism, psychology and management consulting. These merged disciplines provide the theoretical and experiential foundation of her consulting firm, Leadership Development Forum, which specializes in customized leadership development services for senior executives and high potential employees. As a teacher, coach and strategist, Dr. Wasylyshyn has distinguished her work on three fronts: (1) executive coaching, (2) the design and implementation of leadership succession processes, and (3) advancing the application of emotional intelligence in business.

Dr. Wasylyshyn, a licensed psychologist, began her career as a journalist in the publishing industry. She combines this business experience with her clinical training to create practical applications of psychology in business. Typically, her work involves long-term collaborations with senior executives and human resources professionals on issues of leadership effectiveness.

A frequent speaker on the subject of executive development, Dr. Wasylyshyn has coached hundreds of executives representing every global sector. She was honored by Hahnemann University as "Alumna of the Year" for her application of psychology in business, and received similar recognition from the Institute of Graduate Clinical Psychology at Widener University in 2002.

Dr. Wasylyshyn's clients include or have included Bristol Myers Squibb, Campbell Soup, Colgate Palmolive, Dupont, FMC, GE Aerospace, Glaxo-SmithKline, Henkels & McCoy, Johnson and Higgins (now MARSH), Johnson & Johnson, Norfolk Southern Corporation, PECO, Pfizer Int'l, PriceWaterhouseCoopers, Revlon, Rohm and Haas Company (now Dow), Sunbeam, U.S. Steel, and The Vanguard Group.

Her board activities have included The Painted Bride Arts Center, The Girl Scouts of Southeastern Pennsylvania, Womens Way, The Opera Company of Philadelphia, Leadership, Inc., and The Farmers Market Trust. Currently she is Vice Chair of the Widener University Board of Trustees and is an Executive Committee member of the SE Pennsylvania Chapter

K.M. Wasylyshyn, *Behind the Executive Door: Unexpected Lessons for Managing Your Boss and Career*, DOI 10.1007/978-1-4614-0376-0, © Karol M. Wasylyshyn 2012

Board of the American Red Cross. She is a former Board President of The Forum of Executive Women.

Dr. Wasylyshyn's current academic appointment is Adjunct Professor of Clinical Psychology, Institute for Graduate Clinical Psychology at Widener University. She is also a past member of the coaching faculty in The Wharton School's Advanced Management Program. She has lectured ("Coaching at the Top") in a Wharton executive coaching program. In 2000, she established The Center for Applied Emotional Competence at Widener University and has been piloting the use of emotional intelligence in recruiting. A recognized pioneer of executive coaching, her publications focus on best practices and methodological considerations, as well as on individual behavior as a critical dimension of leadership effectiveness. With recent writing and consultation, she has pioneered the use of original poetry to open deeper considerations of leadership behavior.

Epilogue

BEHIND THE EXECUTIVE DOOR highlights the behavior of people who occupy senior leadership roles in business organizations. It provides a psychological understanding of why leaders behave in the ways they do, and it presents a specific continuum of three leadership types – *Remarkable*, *Perilous* and *Toxic*. Executives are seen as moving along this behavioral continuum depending on the confluence of work and personal factors versus being statically locked into any one particular type.

The identification of these leadership types helps objectify the highly subjective nature of leadership behavior by providing a common language – apt, applicable, and memorable language – about leaders in terms of *how* they lead. This understanding influences an efficient starting point or coalescent framing for decisions related to the hiring, development, financial rewarding, and/or promotion of top executives – decisions that in this era of intense behavioral scrutiny must focus equally on both the *what* and *how* dimensions of leadership.

The *unexpected lessons* of BEHIND THE EXECUTIVE DOOR, while psychologically-based, are imminently accessible, pragmatic, and riveted on helping employees manage bosses who represent the *Remarkable*, *Perilous*, and *Toxic* types. In other words, accurate recognition of a boss's leader behavior type can inform the in-the-moment behavior adjustments direct reports may need to make, i.e., their application of various *unexpected lessons* they can apply to manage their bosses more effectively. Managing bosses more effectively bears potentially powerful effects for sound career management.

The over-arching *unexpected lesson* for managing a *Remarkable* boss is channeling the power of reciprocal engagement on issues related to strategy, driving results, managing people and executive credibility. Employees reporting to a *Perilous* boss will be rewarded by efforts to diminish or at least neutralize the boss's sense of unrequited work, i.e., chronic sense of discontentment as related to career accomplishments. People with *Toxic* bosses are wise to conduct a serious appraisal of whether or not they need to remain in a dysfunctional work environment. If so, then peerage is the key boss management lesson – peerage that includes adequate communication, unity, explicit reinforcement of each other's capabilities, and proactive problem-solving to help minimize the chaos and/or craziness that *Toxic* leaders typically unleash in their organizations. If not, then planning one's escape becomes the key lesson to employ.

Finally, in the context of thinking about one's own leadership or leadership potential, remember that you are not consistently one of these leader types and that your special gift to whomever you lead – or love – is to strive to be *Remarkable* most of the time. Is it possible then that these *unexpected lessons* for managing bosses – reciprocity, minimizing discontent, peerage, and escape – might have enduring implications for managing our personal relationships as well?

Appendix A

Based on the *Leadership Type Exercise* (in Chap. 5) the set of statements in which you gave the boss the most checks indicates his/her most frequently occurring leadership TYPE.

First Set of Statements = the *Perilous* Boss

My boss:

___ Has a leadership style that is based primarily on the objective analysis of facts and data; the people issues are a necessary part, too – but a distant second.

___ Forms strong strategies and a compelling picture of the future but getting people excited and aligned about what he/she sees is the hard part.

___ Can keep adjusting his/her thoughts even after a path forward on an issue has been decided; there could be better consistency between what he/she says and does.

___ Thinks he/she is quite self-aware and tuned into him/herself emotionally but he/she gets feedback to the contrary.

___ Believes he/she does a good job of using both positive and negative emotions but after team meetings, for example, people can feel deflated by his/her criticism or missed opportunities for him/her to pump up the team.

___ Will not let organizational politics or other culture factors get in the way of achieving business results.

___ Knows emotional intelligence is a focus in leadership thinking now but he/she is not focused on being empathic about others' concerns.

___ Has work relationships that are primarily transactional, i.e., they're more about getting things done than forming personal ties.

___ Believes empowerment needs to be earned; once people have earned it, then he/she is more willing to delegate fully to them.

___ Sets a course of action, and doesn't like being second-guessed on it.

___ Doesn't like ambiguity – unless it's the ambiguity he/she has created.

___Can show some degree of anxiety or uncertainty when he/she gets new and/or expanded responsibility because he/she needs to feel a sense of mastery and control to lead effectively.

___Is more focused on work/career than on personal relationships.

___Expects people to work out the conflicts that can crop up so his/her intervention is not needed.

___Favors working independently but is OK working with the team.

Second Set of Statements = the *Remarkable* Boss

My boss:

___Forms a strategy for the business or functional area he/she is leading and prefers to do this with his/her leadership team.

___Drives high-quality results in a cost-effective and timely manner.

___Gets the right people in the right roles and sets the conditions for them to be successful.

___Gives a lot of positive feedback and motivational support to direct reports.

___Will always do the right thing even if that means jeopardizing his/her career.

___Spends time planning how best to communicate with employees at all levels in the organization about our strategy and the objectives that must be met to achieve the strategy.

___Expects bold action of him/herself and values this in others. Prefers people ask for forgiveness – not permission.

___Is more focused on leveraging his/her strengths than worrying too much about his/her weaknesses.

___Will spend at least as much time trying to win people's hearts as trying to win their minds.

___Makes a real effort to find out what others are concerned about and their aspirations as well.

___Expects people to be accountable so it's easy for him/her to delegate fully.

___Builds and motivates high-performing teams; this is one of his/her top skills as a leader.

___Forms deep and lasting relationships with people inside and outside the company.

Third Set of Statements = the Toxic Boss

My boss:

___Sometimes acts like business success would be a lot easier if it weren't for the people who need to be lead.

___Is more intuitive than strategic.

___ Can create chaos and there can be a lack of consistency between what he/she says and does.

___ Doesn't focus on other people's feelings about their work or things going on in their lives; probably wouldn't know what to do with that kind of information.

___ Thinks people waste time on company politics and organizational culture issues.

___ When it comes to something like empathy, he/she expects people to get into his/her shoes once in a while.

___ Could be better at delegation but this is hard because he/she believes no one's going to do things as well as he/she would do it.

___ Believes high-performing teams get the job done – they don't need retreats or other team-building experiences to make them effective.

___ Values work as the most important thing in life. Getting close to other people is just not his/her thing.

___ Can be stubborn once he/she has set a course of action. People can bring him/her data supporting a different view but if his/her gut says "no," it's going to be no.

___ Doesn't sleep well when he/she gets a new job. His/her fears about failure can return with a vengeance.

___ Is basically a conflict avoider. He/she doesn't have the time, patience, or skill to deal with negative issues effectively. This has adverse effects on productive team work.

Appendix B

Doing Demon Quiz

1	I spend at least 90% of my time at work getting things done.	True	False
2	I measure my success at work by what I accomplish.	True	False
3	I rarely have quality time to think about and plan for the future needs of my business/company.	True	False
4	I'm known as one of the top "go-to" people in my company. If something important needs to get done, I'm likely to be leading it or at least be involved in it.	True	False
5	I like to turn people's good ideas into processes that make things happen more easily and efficiently.	True	False
6	I have had bosses who said I'm more tactical than strategic.	True	False
7	I have missed out on a promotion because I'm not perceived as a "big picture" thinker.	True	False

Scoring: If you answered four or more of these questions "true," you have a stronger preference for *doing* versus *planning, influencing,* or *having strategic impact.* If you aspire to executive leadership roles, too much tactical "doing" could be a career-limiting factor.

Appendix C

Using A.R.T. to Achieve Peak Performance from Others

Articulate, React, Teach

A Articulate – Bosses provide clear and consistent statements about business strategy, strategic objectives, and time frames for what is to happen when. They also articulate clarity about people's roles, key responsibilities, and delegated tasks.

This is a continuous process of *reciprocal articulation* between bosses and the people who work for them. This requires direct reports to repeat back what they understand about strategy, priorities, timeframes, roles, responsibilities, and delegated work. Through this reverse paraphrasing, any misunderstanding can be caught – and corrected – before there are breakdowns in meeting expectations.

AT ITS BEST, THIS IS A CONTINUOUS PROCESS OF <u>RECIPROCAL ARTICULATION</u> BETWEEN BOSSES AND SUBORDINATES.

R React – Bosses establish a collaborative atmosphere for gauging progress on goals. Once objectives have been delegated, subordinates receive, as needed, constructive input, technical guidance, and positive reinforcement. In addition, the ongoing engagement of the boss is sustained, so when/if initiatives go awry, timely course corrections can be made. Celebrations and rewards of successful outcomes are leveraged for motivational effects.

This is a process of *reciprocal reaction* between bosses and direct reports. It requires direct reports to keep bosses current on the progress of objectives, to signal problems, and to allow sufficient time if adjustments need to be made before deadline dates arrive.

AT ITS BEST, THIS IS AN EMPOWERED PROCESS OF <u>RECIPROCAL REACTION</u> BETWEEN BOSSES AND SUBORDINATES.

T Teach – Bosses engage people in continuous learning often using the de-briefing of both successful and unsuccessful objectives as a key learning tool. Each party in the boss–subordinate dyad remains committed to new learning as a central proposition for continued success and maintaining competitive advantage.

This is an open atmosphere characterized by mutual respect, lack of defensiveness, and excitement about learning from each others' mistakes and successes.

AT ITS BEST, THIS IS A CHALLENGING PROCESS OF <u>RECIPROCAL TEACHING</u> BETWEEN BOSSES AND SUBORDINATES.

Appendix D

Emotional Intelligence (EQ) for Recruitment
Sample questions based on the four EQ dimensions (SO SMART®)

SO Self-observation

Tell us about a time when the use of your emotions had a positive effect on the outcome of an important issue at work.

Describe a work-related situation when your emotional reaction had an adverse effect on an important objective.

What did you learn from this?

SM Self-management

Give us an example of when things were tense, pitched, or contentious at work but you were able to channel your emotions well.

Tell us about a time when you really didn't control your emotions so well – a time when, in retrospect, you even regretted how you reacted.

What was the key learning for you from this?

A Attunement

Tell us about a work-related situation when your empathy or ability to "tune into" others made a difference in an outcome.

Give us an example of a time when you missed important behavioral signals from someone and how that had a negative effect on something you were trying to accomplish.

How would you handle this type of situation now?

RT Relationship Traction

Give us an example of you at your persuasive and influential best.

Tell us about a time when you were NOT as persuasive and influential as you needed to be. How would you handle this type of situation now?

How would people who are or who have worked with you recently describe their relationships with you?

Appendix E

A Tool for Assessing Team Members

RESULTS (R)/BEHAVIOR GRID (B)	
+R +B	−R +B
+R −B	−R −B

Upper left quadrant
- The "high potential" people.
- Both RESULTS and BEHAVIOR are strong.

- Major question:

  - "What do we need to do to keep them energized?"

Upper right quadrant
- The "question marks."
- RESULTS are not where they need to be but BEHAVIOR is right; usually highly loyal people.

- Major questions:

  - How much time does this person need to get up to speed? (When person is new to role).
  - Will this person ever be able to get up to speed? (When person has been in the role for awhile).
  - If the situation is fixable, what do we need to do to get the results on track (training, coaching, etc.)?

Lower left quadrant
- The "saboteurs."

- RESULTS are strong but BEHAVIOR is a real problem; these people can be high maintenance, sour others with their cynicism and/or aggression, or otherwise erode consistent team performance or positive morale.

- **Major questions:**
  - Is a behavior adjustment possible? If so, what needs to happen for that adjustment to occur (e.g. coaching)?
  - If behavior adjustment is not possible, is he/she more trouble than he/she is worth? If no, then retain person but step up performance management and make sure awards are aligned. If yes, remove person from team as soon as feasible, or place individual in individual contributor role, if possible.

Lower right quadrant
- The "dead wood" OR "recyclables."
- RESULTS and BEHAVIOR are both negative.

- **Major questions:**
  - Is this a temporary thing? If so, how quickly can an adjustment occur?
  - What needs to happen for an adjustment to occur? If it's not just a flukey, temporary thing, is there another role in the organization in which this person can be successful? If so, make it happen. If not, clear the way for a dignified exit.

NOTE: When the problem is a wrong role and there is a right role for the person, he/she has the potential to move into the upper left ("high potential") quadrant.

Appendix F

Career Management Resources

George Dow
Principal
George Dow Consulting, LLC
5200 Willson Road, Suite 150
Edina, MN 55424
952-836-2792
george@georgedow.com

Barbara Gronsky, Ph.D.
Principal
Delaware Valley Career Solutions, LLC
1601 Walnut Street, Suite 901
Philadelphia, PA 19102
215-504-9600
bgronsky@delawarevalleycareersolutions.com

Gerald Mosely, PhD
Principal
Career Development Coaching
4618 Village Green Drive
El Dorado Hills, CA 95762
916-549-3719
ghmosley@gmail.com

Douglas B. Richardson, JD, MA
Partner
Edge International US, LLC
1325 Hollow Road
Penn Valley, PA 19072
610-660-9555
richardson@edge-international.com

Jeremy Robinson, MSW, MCC
Principal
Robinson Capital Corp.
201 West 74 Street, Suite # 14F
New York, New York 10023
cell: 917-903-3526
office: 212-501-8991
ceocoachrobinson@gmail.com

Mitch Wienick
President/CEO
Kelleher Associates
Four Glenhardie Corporate Center
Wayne, PA 19087-1565
610-293-1115
MWienick@Kelleherllc.com

References

Argyris, C. (1991). Teaching smart people how to learn. *Harvard Business Review, 69*(May–June), 99–109.

Boyatzis, R., & Goleman, D. (2008). Social intelligence and the biology of leadership. *Harvard Business Review, 136,* 87–92.

Braddick, C., & Braddick, G. (2003). *The ROI (return on investment) of executive coaching: Useful information or a distraction? Part 2 of a 2 part series.* Retrieved January 5, 2004, from www.ukhrd.com.

Brienza, D., & Cavallo, K. (2005). Emotional competence and leadership excellence at Johnson & Johnson: The emotional intelligence and leadership study. *The Consortium for Research on Emotional Intelligence in Organizations.* Retrieved July 9, 2008, from www.eiconsortium.org.

Bryant, A. (2010). Good C.E.O.'s are insecure (and know it). *New York Times.* Retrieved from http://www.nytimes.com/2010/10/10/business/10corner. html.

Collins, J. (2001). *Good to great.* New York: HarperCollins.

Druskat, V. U., & Wolff, S. B. (2001). Building the emotional intelligence of groups. *Harvard Business Review,* 81–90.

DePree, M. (1989). *Leadership is an art.* New York: Dell.

Ghaemi, N. (2011). *A first-rate madness: Uncovering the links between leadership and mental illness.* New York: The Penguin Press.

Goleman, D., & Boyatzis, R. (2008). Social intelligence and the biology of leadership. *Harvard Business Review,* 2–8.

Goleman, D. (1996). *Emotional intelligence.* New York: Bantam Books.

Goleman, D. (1998). What makes a leader? *Harvard Business Review, 76,* 93–102.

Goleman, D., Boyatzis, R., & McKee, A. (2002). *Primal leadership: Realizing the power of emotional intelligence.* Boston: Harvard Business School Press.

Groysberg, B., Kelly, L. K., & MacDonald, B. (2011). The new path to the c-suite. *Harvard Business Review, 89*(3), 60–68.

Kaplan, R. E., & Kaiser, R. B. (2003). Developing versatile leadership. *MIT Sloan Management Review, 44*(4), 19–26.

Korn, M. (2011). As the world turns, Wharton adapts. *The Wall Street Journal.* Retrieved from http://online.wsj.com/article.

Lombardo, M., & Eichinger, R. (1992). *The career architect version 2.2 c [portfolio sort cards].* Minneapolis: Lominger.

Maccoby, M. (1976). *The Gamesman: The new corporate leaders.* New York: Simon and Schuster.

Maccoby, M. (2000). Narcissistic leaders: The incredible pros, the inevitable cons. *Harvard Business Review, 78*(1), 69–77.

Mayer, J., Roberts, R., & Barsade, S. (2008). Human abilities: Emotional intelligence. *Annual Review of Psychology, 59,* 507–536.

McAdams, D. P. (2006). The redemptive self: Generativity and the stories Americans live by. *Research in Human Development, 3*(2–3), 81–100.

McKnight, R., Kaney, T., & Breuer, S. (2010). *Leading strategy execution: How to align the senior team, design a strategy-capable organization, and get all employees on-board.* Philadelphia: TrueNorth Press.

Rifkin, J. (2009). *The empathic civilization: The race to global consciousness in a world in crisis.* New York: Jeremy P. Tarcher/Penguin.

Rock, D. (2010). Impacting leadership with neuroscience. *People & Strategy, 33*(4), 6–7.

Ronson, J. (2011). *The psychopath test: A journey through the madness industry.* New York: Riverhead Books.

Rosenberg, A. (2011). *Wilson Goode finds peace in the pulpit. Philadelphia Inquirer.* http://articles.philly.com/2011-01-17/news/27033157_1_pulpit-wilson-goode-god.

Rotter, J. B. (1954). *Social learning and clinical psychology.* New York: Prentice-Hall.

Stefano, S. F., & Wasylyshyn, K. M. (2005). Integrity, courage, empathy (ICE): Three leadership essentials. *Human Resource Planning, 28*(4).

Triandis, H. C. (1993). Collectivism and individualism as cultural syndromes. *Cross-Cultural Research, 27,* 155–180.

Wasylyshyn, K. M. (2003). Coaching the superkeepers. In L. A. Berger & D. R. Berger (Eds.), *The talent management handbook: Creating organizational excellence through identifying developing and positioning your best people.* New York: McGraw-Hill.

Wasylyshyn, K. M. (2010). Avoiding bad hires: Using emotional intelligence as a selection tool. *Journal of Psychological Issues in Organizational Cultures, 1–3,* 319–330.

Wasylyshyn, K. M. (2011a). *Standing on marbles: Three leader types in verse and imagery.* Philadelphia: TrueNorth Press.

Wasylyshyn, K. M. (2011b). Developing top talent: Guiding principles, methodology and practice considerations. In L. A. Berger & D. R. Berger (Eds.), *The talent management handbook* (2nd ed.). New York: McGraw-Hill.

Welch, J. (2004). Four e's (a jolly good fellow). *Wall Street Journal, A14.*

Whyte, D. (1994). *The heart aroused: Poetry and the preservation of the soul in corporate America.* New York: Doubleday.

Index